Confessions of a
BAPTIST MINISTER

JON MAGEE

authorHOUSE

AuthorHouse™ UK
1663 Liberty Drive
Bloomington, IN 47403 USA
www.authorhouse.co.uk
Phone: UK TFN: 0800 0148641 (Toll Free inside the UK)
UK Local: (02) 0369 56322 (+44 20 3695 6322 from outside the UK)

© 2024 Jon Magee. All rights reserved.

No part of this book may be reproduced, stored in a retrieval system, or transmitted by any means without the written permission of the author.

Published by AuthorHouse 09/05/2024

ISBN: 979-8-8230-8916-6 (sc)
ISBN: 979-8-8230-8919-7 (e)

Library of Congress Control Number: 2024916916

Print information available on the last page.

Any people depicted in stock imagery provided by Getty Images are models, and such images are being used for illustrative purposes only.
Certain stock imagery © Getty Images.

This book is printed on acid-free paper.

Because of the dynamic nature of the Internet, any web addresses or links contained in this book may have changed since publication and may no longer be valid. The views expressed in this work are solely those of the author and do not necessarily reflect the views of the publisher, and the publisher hereby disclaims any responsibility for them.

Contents

Foreword		ix
Introduction		xi
Chapter 1	Admin and the door to prayer.	1
Chapter 2	The call, and the answer	6
Part 1	The African Experience	6
Part 2	Being a witness	14
Part 3	The Next Step	15
Part 4	Faith	17
Chapter 3	Assurance of a call	23
Chapter 4	Matches and Dispatches	30
Part 1	Dispatches	30
Part 2	Matches	38
Chapter 5	Facing the elements	49
Part 1	Flight into the unknown	49
Part 2	Lesson in Faith from the Fishermen	55
Chapter 6	Veterans of the past	57
Part 1	Destroy or rebuild?	57
Part 2	The Wisdom of Willy	63
Chapter 7	Prison Ministry	64

Chapter 8	Ministry to all	73
Chapter 9	Taking the opportunities.	86
Part 1	The ultimate Questions	86
Part 2	The singer or the Song	90
Part 3	Barren Rocks or Living Stones?	93
Chapter 10	Practical suggestions in effective ministry	98
Part 1	Being full and overflowing?	98
Part 2	Disruptions in the service?	101
Part 3	Knowing the community	103
Part 4	Knowing the people.	107
Part 5	Being a prayerful encouragement but never a discouraging critic.	109
Part 6	Listen to the doctor orders.	112
Part 7	Try Praying!	115
Part 8	Can the World see the work of God?	118
Part 9	Never write a person off as being impossible	120
Part 10	Back to the future	121
Chapter 11	Going the extra mile	124
Part 1	Ben Vicar	124
Part 2	Kildalton	127
Part 3	Reaching the unreachable	131
Part 4	Mary	134
Part 5	Compassion Regardless	135
Part 6	Genuine care	136
Part 7	God turned it into good	138
Chapter 12	Lock Down or Break Out?	140
Part 1	Finance	140
Part 2	Fellowship	141
Part 3	Zoom	142
Part 4	YouTube	143

Part 5	Radio	145
Part 6	The return	146
Chapter 13	Come together	148
Chapter 14	Expect the unexpected	153
Part 1	The unexpected flowers	153
Part 2	The bomb!	154
Part 3	Hearse driving	156
Chapter 15	Partnership Missions	158
Chapter 16	Preaching in America	165
Part 1	Childs perspective	166
Part 2	The corner where the devil hides!I	167
Part 3	Opportunity	170
Part 4	Feeling the heat.	171
Part 5	Watch your language!	173
Part 6	Take time	175
Conclusion		179

Foreword

Firstly, this book is like a string of pearls. Jon is the cord that joins them all together, each pearl is a person. Some of these people were on their own journey and crossed Jon's path, others were people like Baden Powell who influenced Jon's approach to that journey. Secondly, it is confessional in the way it is delivered. Jon is very honest, conveying to the reader his deepest thoughts and emotions, including acknowledging his own mistakes or errors of judgement. The stories within are humorous, heart breaking, inspirational, unique and totally human. Faith in Jesus is the golden thread running through each chapter.

Rev. David Kinder

Former Lead Chaplain, Littlehey Prison.

Introduction

It was Saturday the 5th March 1983. A date that I can never forget. That date is an important milestone in my life as I was inducted into my first full time ministry at Bowmore and Port Ellen on the island of Islay in the Hebrides. (At that time they were constituted as two completely autonomous churches which shared the one Minister.) Just a week before that I was ordained at my home church, Springburn Baptist Church in Glasgow. These people in Glasgow and Islay played an important role in those formative years of my ministry which has now lasted for the next 41 years. Those early years were years of inexperience for me, but God was going to fill them up with the experience of God through His people.

Moses began his main career at the age of 80, and what a tremendous career it was. However, in all honesty I consider that it is unlikely that I will see another 41 years. It seems to me that this is the time to put in writing a record of the work of God during these years. It is a God who continues to be faithful, a God that we can trust to walk with us in all we do in His name.

I mentioned the 5th March 1983. It is fairly obvious when I say the following day was Sunday the 6th March. We stood on the pier at Port Ellen to say farewell to those who had come to support me on this important weekend. As the ferry arrived disaster came with it. The ferry came in too far to one side and struck a sand bank. For those unused to sea travel you could see the look of fear that was on their faces. However, all was not lost no matter how disastrous it may appeared to have been. The local fishermen came to the rescue and pulled the ferry to its rightful place. That was quite an interesting sight to see as all these small fishing boats tied to the larger ferry boat that they were rescuing. Some may see it as an omen of the dreadful times ahead following the induction. For me, it was a reminder that no matter how big the disaster there is a God who will come to our rescue.

I hope that you enjoy the read. For those who are involved in public speaking you are welcome to use any of the pages of this book as illustrations as you talk. May God richly bless you in your own journey of life.

Jon Magee
July 2024

Chapter 1

Admin and the door to prayer.

My youth was noted as being very nomadic and, due to the reasons of being nomadic, often it was a turbulent life living in places of conflict. My father served in the British Royal Air Force as a Medical Secretary, and so did I for ten years as an Electronic Technician working on aircraft communications. This has included HF, VHF and UHF radio and also radio navigational aids. So by the time I reached the age of thirty I had never lived anywhere more than three years maximum, and was educated in fourteen schools by the time I had completed my secondary education. In addition, due to the security concerns in one country where we lived when I was at a vital stage of my secondary education I had no school for a whole term. Formal education was always a catch up game, but there were other factors that moved me forward that can never be gleaned from a text book.

The result of my nomadic youth is that I have lived through many of the major milestones of late 20th century history. In the 1950's I was in Singapore as a child, in the Far East, during the Chinese riots. From 1960 to 1962 I was in Germany at the height of the Cold War. We were based on a small secret Radar station, a listening post for all that was happening in the

Soviet Union and Eastern Europe, so there was an awareness that if the cold war had thawed in any way we would soon be on the front line, and as such we needed to always keep alert. In 1966 and 1967 I was in Aden (in the south of what is now Yemen at the entrance to the Red Sea). I was a teenager living in the midst of the conflict and terrorism of the time and the British evacuation in 1967. As an adult, having joined the RAF, I arrived in Malta as the Maltese Prime Minister, Don Mintoff, decided he did not like the British, and then I went to Cyprus with my new wife, Joan, from 1973 till 1975, just in time for the Military coup and Turkish invasions of 1974.

(Please note that "invasion" is a military term and refers to one country entering another country with military force. This certainly happened irrespective of whether one takes any sides or not. The term "intervention" currently used by Turkey would not have been possible if the Turkish government had not entered by military force, as was my experience)

So, following such a life as that, what are the options that might lie ahead having left the RAF? Become a Baptist Minister? What a peaceful life it must be in comparison. At least that is what some folks may think. As for the truth? For some people I guess that there is no point in letting the truth get in the way of a good story. In reality I would suggest that the experiences of my youth were good preparation for what I believe was to be the call of God in my life.

So what is the true story? Let me begin with one of my first Church Business meetings. Nothing can go wrong with that. It was just the humdrum boring stuff that needed to be discussed, just the basics of the replacement of an external door. Being in the Hebrides inevitably means that these external parts of a building face some rugged and rough handling. The islands that are on the Western edge of the British Isles offer some great extremes – not only of interesting sights throughout the year but also of the weather. The Hebrides are regularly exposed to the extremes of wind and rain but, relatively speaking, enjoy a mild climate, with frosts being rare.

Not only can you experience all four seasons in one day here; by standing on a headland in sunshine watching hail across the sea, and it can feel as though you can experience them all at once. So, while snow and frost are relatively rare, gale force winds are not at all uncommon. Like in other parts of western Scotland, the weather can sometimes be very changeable. With nothing in between the Isle of Islay, where the church concerned is situated, and the east coast of Canada and America, except the huge Atlantic Ocean, the south-westerly winds are an almost constant factor. On a positive note, a saying on Islay about the weather is "If you don't like the weather, wait five minutes". It can change. Yet for all of that the extremes of weather can bring a need for this door to be discussed. It needed to be replaced without a doubt, it had come to the end of its natural life.

The meeting was very business like. It was decided that there should be three quotes provided and the church should go with the best quote that happened to be provided. That seems to be quite straight forward. No problem. In time the quotes were returned. We gathered together once more and considered them all. One of them stood out as being an amazing quote that was given. I was impressed. The quote was given by a man known as "Big John". (I have altered the name for reasons that will soon become evident) As we looked at the quotes someone observed that "Big John" was a really remarkable joiner and that he could do a tremendous job creating a door. His quote was also the lowest out of the three that were offered, and on the basis of our previous decision there is no doubt that he should have the job. However, he also had a reputation which was that once he started drinking you never knew when the work would be completed. So, sadly, it was decided not to give him the job.

A few days passed by and "Big John" was knocking at my door. I instantly realised that "big" was certainly an accurate description of the man as I determined how I might best respond to his petition, and yes, he had been drinking. It was a long stone flight of stairs he needed to climb to reach our front door and I wondered how he managed to get to the top without falling. It must have been quite a challenge for him under the influence of the drink. I looked up at this giant of a man who towered over me. He was desperate for the job. He pleaded for the work as he explained that we would never find a better craftsman on the island than himself, which I had already heard about. In addition, he said, whoever was the lowest quote he promised he would undercut them and still provide an excellent job. On the face of it that seems like a good proposition. How do I tell him that his was the lowest quote? I decided that was not the best approach, but rather I apologised and said that though I am the Minister I do not have the final say on such decisions. I guess that is hard for the average person outside the church to understand, but that is the reality. Eventually "Big John" moved on, and I assumed that was the end of the matter. Now I can relax, I thought. I breathed a sigh of relief.

Later in the same day a member of the church approached me. "Jon, did I see Big John at your door earlier today?" I agreed that was the case. "Oh, he must have had the gun in his pocket when he spoke with you then". That was a huge shock for me as you can imagine. Apparently he had gone straight from my door walking down Main Street turning right along Shore street and then walked into the Bank of Scotland, pulled a gun out of his pocket and demanded that the Teller hand over the money. While he spoke with me the risks were clearly all there, yet I never had a clue. I am convinced the Lord was overlooking me that day ensuring my personal protection. He knew my need before I realised it and I am so thankful.

This was an important lesson that I learnt early in my ministry, even in the triviality of church administration everything needs to be undergirded in prayer. I would hope that church members would also learn to pray that decisions they make in a church meeting need to come with the wisdom of God.

Prayer isn't just about asking God for things you need or desire. It's about establishing a relationship with God that is built on faith and trust in Him. God knows the desires of your heart long before you even think to ask, but he still loves to hear from you, whether you're asking for guidance or giving thanks, because it draws you closer to him. The Bible is full of people who were led to pray for a multitude of things we still pray about today, such as fear, anger, worry. That's why the Good Book is chock-full of Bible verses about worry, strength, and hope. When you're questioning just how effective prayer really is, these Bible verses will help motivate you to get down on your knees and communicate with the Lord. As such, is it any wonder that I speak here about the importance of prayer even in the mundane issues of ministry. Whatever may be our concerns in the realm of worry and strength, when we can communicate with our God we can discover our hope even before we realise our need for it. That was certainly the experience I had on that day with "Big John".

The Psalmist discovered this truth when he declared "Answer me when I call, O God of my righteousness! You have given me relief when I was in distress. Be gracious to me and hear my prayer!" (Psalm 4 verse 1)

Chapter 2

The call, and the answer

Part 1
The African Experience

There is so much more to add, but let's take a break as I now share how God called me into Pastoral ministry.

I am the youngest of six siblings, though as I write there are only four of us that are still surviving. From a young age I had gone to church with my family but my personal commitment was far from what it really should be. I had religion and ritual but I did not fully understand that it was a relationship I needed, a relationship with Jesus. I had spoken of sensing a call from God from quite a young age and many assumed that revealed my Christian commitment, but I never gave a real positive response to that call. I believe a response to the call is important, and I had failed in that aspect of the relationship that our Lord desires each of us to have with Him. The loving relationship that our Lord desires for us to know was completely one sided in my case. I knew the reality of what the bible says in John chapter 3, that God so loved the world, including myself, that He gave His only begotten son that whoever believes in Him will not perish but will have everlasting life. What a great sacrifice Jesus Christ made for me! He is the one that had taken the initiative, not myself. Where was my love for the Lord in return? It was not there!

It was as a teenager during a three week visit to Kenya, Africa, that things began to make sense for me. I had been living in Aden, in the south of what is now known as Yemen, at the entrance to the Red Sea. The church we attended at RAF Khormaksar, Aden, was organising a working holiday for the men to Kenya, and I was joining the party as the youngest member. Living on an RAF base it was planned that we would hitch a lift on a regular RAF flight going in that direction. So it was in 1966 that I arrived at the Kenyan Air Force station at Eastleigh, just outside Nairobi. It was formerly known as RAF Eastleigh prior to independence when Kenya was still a British colony and is located to the east of Nairobi, in the Eastleigh suburb. I was one of a number of men going on this working holiday to a Methodist Mission station at Meru on the foothills of Mount Kenya, just above the equator. Following an overnight stay at the CMS guest house in Nairobi we began our journey north in a hired car. As a British teenage school boy this seemed to me like a dream come true, to spend three weeks in "Darkest Africa". That is a term that was initially used about Africa not in any racist intention but rather that it was dark because it was so unknown. For myself in the 20th century it was still unknown yet ironically it was to be the means of bringing some light into my own life. It was with a sense of excitement that I envisaged the exploration of this new environment for me. Whilst in Nairobi we felt like the scene was being set as we went to a Drive through cinema to see "Born Free" which had been filmed nearby. However, the excitement I envisaged could never compare with the reality of the spiritual experience I was about to discover.

On the route to Meru we passed through Nyeri in the Central Highlands of Kenya. From my scouting experience the very name of the town struck a chord for me. Nyeri hosts the tomb of Lord Baden Powell, the founder of the Scouting movement, who died on the 8th January 1941. After retirement, in 1938, this is the town where he had made his home. We stopped in the town and made our way to St Peter's cemetery where we found his grave. I was fascinated by the inscriptions on the grave stone. Following the usual details of his name and the dates of his birth and death there was something more. His gravestone bore a circle with a dot in the centre "⊙", which I recognised instantly as the trail sign for "Going home", or "I have gone home". What a message to declare at this time. Death does not need to be the end, but the beginning of a new chapter of life when we know with confidence where we are going. Gone home! Is that a message I can declare for me, I thought to myself. I was not so sure that it was.

As we continued our journey we crossed the equator. We knew we had reached that global point as there was a sign post marking it on the side of the road along with information about the altitude of where we were standing. For some reason it did not make such a huge impression on me at the time. A spiritual warmth was still to arrive in my life, far more than being on the equator where most would expect to have a lot of heat. In reality, due to the altitude and also that we were already acclimatised to the heat in Aden it was not as hot as one would expect.

Our journey needed to progress further, making our way through the foothills of Mount Kenya till we reached the town of Meru on the North east slope of the mountain. It was a town predominantly populated by the Ameru people, a Bantu ethnic group. Swahili is the most widely spoken African language in Sub-Saharan Africa. It is the national language of Kenya but in addition there were many tribal languages in Africa including that of the Ameru people. The word Meru itself means 'shining light' in the Meru language, another reminder for myself of the lack of a spiritual light in my own life as I spent three weeks in this town of "shining light".

Like many countries in Africa, Kenya is abundant in mammals, birds, reptiles, and insects. With regard to insects one of our team was to have an unpleasant and unforgettable experience as man eating ants began to climb his leg. He was fortunate that young native boys saw his predicament and acted quickly to remove the risks that invaded his space. Many iconic wildlife species of Africa are native to Kenya, including lions, hippos, elephants, buffalo, zebras, and giraffes. I felt it was a privilege to be able to see some of these animals for the first time in their natural habitat. One of the many reasons some people come to visit Kenya is to see its amazing and unique wildlife up close. That was not part of the initial plan for me when I visited Kenya, but I found it to be a wonderful bonus. Kenya was a dream safari territory, a place where you can watch leopards slink through the tall grass, lions laze in the shade of acacia trees and huge elephant herds trundling across the wide-open dusty plains. Yes, I had seen some of these animals in zoo's back in England, but here the animals were free. It is freedom that many humans will prize as a quality to be desired, and likewise for these animals they deserve to have their own sense of freedom.

I remember specifically seeing giraffe's living and roaming in their natural habitat. We saw them in the distance and hoped to see them at close range, so we parked on the roadside hoping to see these graceful animals marked by their noteworthy long necks. These giraffes use their long necks to feed in the tops of the acacia trees, where they gather leaves and fruit. As we followed we saw them feeding in such a way as that. You can usually tell which trees they've feasted on: Since they tend to eat from the top (where the freshest leaves are), the trees tend to look a bit like hats. You'd be hard pressed to find someone who's not intrigued by Giraffes, and we shared that same interest.

As we followed the giraffes, camera's in hand as we sought to capture every possible image, it suddenly dawned on us that we had wandered far from our vehicle. Foolishly, we were so engrossed with following these wonderful animals that we had not given sufficient thought as to how we might get home. We were lost, hopelessly lost. The car was our means of moving on, and we had no idea which way to turn to reach it. We were situated in an environment that was certainly not our natural habitat. This was their world, the world of these African animals, not ours. What were we to do? We talked together and discussed what we could use as a guide. There was just one possibility, the sun. Where was the sun positioned as we left the car, and what direction does it lie in now? This was our guide, our only guide, as we began to walk back. It was a success, we eventually arrived as we hoped. Yet our success was not possible without a reliable guide. Once again I sensed another spiritual reminder in my own life. The sun was the guide moving from the giraffes to the car, but what is my spiritual guide in life? Do I have one?

During one of the weekends that we were in Meru we heard that there were a series of special open air meetings. We were invited to go along, assured that we would find them inspirational. So we went, still unsure of what exactly we would discover when we got there. The area was extremely crowded, full of local people who had, perhaps, been given similar invitations to what was given to ourselves. We were recognised as being amongst the few Europeans in the locality. One young person went out of his way to make us feel at home, which was an encouragement, greeting us in Swahili saying "Jambo", and offering to accompany us whilst we were there. Kenya is known for the friendliness of the Kenyan people, and this is my memory. These young people demonstrated this friendliness to the point of perfection. At one end of the field was a platform that had been erected with a shade placed above those who would be speaking from there. I listened as they spoke, but could not understand a single word they were saying. I realise that the meetings were intended for the local people, so there was no reason why I should expect them to speak in English. Were they speaking in the Meru language or the more national language of Swahili? I did not know, but there was no doubt that the speakers were very charismatic and inspiring in how they spoke and made a huge impression on the listeners who understood the language spoken. Above the platform was a banner with what appeared to be a slogan related to the theme that was impressing the listeners. "Hapana amani kwa waovu, asema BWANA." What could that be about? I turned to my new friend, asking about the banner. The words were in Swahili, it seems, and translates to the words "There is no peace, saith the LORD, unto the wicked", a direct quote from Isaiah chapter 48 verse 22. Peace? Did I know peace? No. Did I need peace? Most certainly. How could I gain this prize that was so important to me? I was still grappling with these vital questions without grasping the answers.

Daily we would make our way each morning to our working project. The team was assigned to the building of a home for a missionary to live in. As the one with least experience in these things I was working more as a labourer, assisting the rest of the team who came with more expertise. Our presence appeared to spark remarkable interest among the local people, particularly among the young. Soon after our arrival at the building in the morning we would see the young people making their way toward us, fascinated by the presence of these Europeans. Other than a few missionaries many of them had never seen Europeans in this part of Africa.

As the days went by we began to expect their arrival, indeed looking forward to seeing them, and to build up a rapport with them. Just up from where we were working we were aware that a family lived in housing that we would never have been used to in Britain. They were typical African round huts, one roomed huts that were cylindrical in shape. They were made from a ring of timber posts, filled in with mud, and topped with a conical thatched roof made with grass and with local materials. We felt honoured that one day a member of the family invited us to their home and to accept their offer of hospitality.

We made our way to where the family lived and received their greetings. Remembering that the huts had only one room the family occupied a number of huts that were set in a circle. As we were shown into one of the huts we lowered our heads as we passed through the low door. The hut had no windows, but there was a ventilation hole left in the top of the roof. We were amazed to discover how cool the buildings were. Mud, a traditional construction material in Africa, more easily keeps the buildings cool compared perhaps with concrete. A simple construction, it seemed, yet it was so effective. We sat on the floor in a circle and awaited the hospitality that they promised to us. They clearly wanted to give us the best of what they would have in their own culture. I remember the first item they brought to us, though I struggle to recall the name they gave to the food. They explained to us that it was like porridge. It was liquidy, made out of maize, cooked over a charcoal fire and tasted of charcoal. No self respecting Scotsman would have called it porridge, but we realised that they were giving from the heart what was special to them and so we ate all that was given in appreciation of their kindness to us.

As I returned to my home in Aden I continued to think about that visit to our Kenyan friends and all that they provided for us. Despite the terrorism that was happening in Aden I knew that I had everything that was important from a western perspective. I lived in a comfortable home with guaranteed healthy meals each day. Everything should be well. My Kenyan friends lived a simple life, in comparison, in a simple mud home and simple meals. Yet there was something about them that was certainly missing from my own life. They clearly knew a peace that I did not have. As I reflected upon this it dawned on me that there was only one reason for this. They had made a commitment to trust Jesus Christ as Saviour and Lord whilst I had not. For me that was the final piece of the jigsaw of my life coming together, completing the overall picture. In the quietness of my own room I discovered that peace for myself as I declared Jesus to be my Lord and Saviour. For me this was the beginning of my Christian life, the beginning of a new and vital relationship with Jesus. This was the vital relationship that I needed to know and to experience. I could have confidence that with this relationship there is a new hope I can know.

Part 2
Being a witness

As I reflect back I would say that I was more of an introvert than an extrovert. I was conscious that the bible had so much to say about witnessing and sharing with others how God had blessed me and given to me this new hope and peace which I had come to know. Yet this was alien to my introverted life. I could not do it. I also knew that the bible speaks of the importance of living in a manner that pleases God, putting into perspective God's lifestyle, so that is what I sought to do. It was as I began to put this into action that I discovered questions were being asked as to why there was this change. I am conscious that when people ask the questions there is a good chance they are interested in discovering the answers. This has to be better than one person giving a monologue. It was also what I considered to be God's answer to my being an introvert. I was saying I cannot do it, but God was opening up a way for it all to happen. It may be true that I cannot do it, but God can. That is a more important perspective. Perhaps I should have learned the lessons from Moses. When God called him to go and speak to Pharaoh Moses said he could not do it, but God found the way and showed it to him. There appeared to be some kind of limitation in his speech but there were no limitations with God.

Every step of my journey as God called me into ministry I always had an objection to what was happening and why I could not possibly do what God had set before me. They were not valid reasons I can see that with hindsight, they were only excuses. I guess we can all have 20/20 vision with anything when we have hindsight. God is a master at giving to us a worthy line in response to our stubborn refusal to be obedient. For me it was a continual reminder of a biblical verse from 1 Peter chapter 5. Each time it came to me from the Authorised Version which can be so much more colourful. Peter wrote " Feed the flock of God which is among you, taking the oversight thereof, not by constraint, but willingly; not for filthy lucre, but of a ready mind" (1 Peter chapter 5 verse 2). Leaving school I joined the RAF without yet responding to God's call into ministry.

Part 3
The Next Step

I recall when I first sensed a call to preach, albeit as a lay person. At that time I was a member of the Methodist church which uses lay preachers more than most churches but giving to the preachers a good process of training. Methodism works on a circuit basis with a Minister covering a number of churches in a circuit, so the support of the lay Preachers is essential if the circuit and local churches were to be able to function adequately. I was aware that there was a need for preachers in the local circuit, and I felt that this was God's calling, yet still I would say "No, I cannot do it." It was hard for me to speak to one or two people so how could I possibly address a room full of people? And God's answer to that? " Feed the flock of God which is among you, taking the oversight thereof, not by constraint, but willingly; not for filthy lucre, but of a ready mind". Eventually I submitted to God's will with reference to the preaching, and amazingly once I stood in the pulpit all my fears melted away. That was an assurance for me that this was indeed God's will.

There was a similar sequence when it came to responding to a call to be a Sunday school teacher and also to share in the leadership of an interdenominational bible study meeting in the Married Quarters of the RAF station where I had been posted. Each time the call of God became apparent I would respond by saying "No, I cannot", as if I knew better than the one I called Lord. Sounds a bit like Peter who had the vision whilst sat on the roof of the house, a vision of unclean food coming down on a sheet and the Lord saying "Get up and eat". Peter also challenged God by saying "Not so Lord". How can we really mean "Lord" and say "Not so" in the same line? If He is my Lord then logically I should be obedient to what He is saying. When I said not so, what did the Lord say to me? " Feed the flock of God which is among you, taking the oversight thereof, not by constraint, but willingly; not for filthy lucre, but of a ready mind"

By this time we were living in Pembrokeshire, Wales. We had two children that were preschool age and a third was on the way. In addition to caring for the children along with Joan I was preaching on average at least one service a week, and teaching in the Sunday school and the bible study as well as doing a full time work in the Royal Air Force. Yet I sensed that the Lord was nudging me to do more. There did not seem to be time to do any more without going into full time ministry, and as usual I always had my excuses as to why I could not possibly manage to do that. I was too young, I thought, and though I had lived in dangerous parts of the world I was too young to know anything about death among those close to me. I did not have that kind of experience that would equip me to be a source of comfort as I would need to be as a full time Minister. Paul wrote "we can comfort those in any trouble with the comfort we ourselves receive from God." (2 Corinthians chapter 1 verse 4) It would seem from what Paul says that I had nothing to give, so how could I minister?

I recalled the time I heard of the death of a man who had been a great encouragement to me in Christian work. He was like a father figure in my life. He had done so much for me, the least I could do was to visit his widow despite my inadequacies. I made my way to the house and knocked on the door. There was no answer. I felt I had done what I should, it could not be my fault that there was no answer, I thought. I wrote a short note, put it through the door, and left. On the Sunday I saw the widow in the church we attended. She said that she could not understand how she never heard me at the door. Her daughter was there with her all day and neither of them had heard a sound. How come they never heard? The answer was really simple, I had knocked so quietly that no one could have possibly heard. I had been through the motions, kidding myself that I had done what was right but in reality I knew I had not. I might say that I have insufficient experience to find ways to bring comfort, little did I know that very soon that was all about to change.

Part 4
Faith

It was just a few months later, having moved to Elgin in the north east of Scotland, and we saw the birth of our third daughter. Like any other family the hopes of new birth was something that we had been looking forward to but we quickly realised as we gathered in the local hospital that all was far from well. We saw the face of the doctor changing dramatically. It was just one week earlier he had been reassuring my wife, Joan, that she was expecting a healthy baby as he listened to what he thought was a very strong heart beat. "One thing is for sure, the baby has the heart as strong as an elephant" the doctor said. Those words could never be forgotten. Nothing could possibly go wrong, he thought, and now he was realising how wrong he was. Later it was to be diagnosed that there was a defective heart valve, so the medical team needed to work fast. We knew that there was a name we needed to cling to in the coming days as the baby was given the name Faith Dawn Marie. We felt so helpless in our human abilities, but we knew we needed to trust in the midst of a very dark time in our lives. The doctor knew that this small hospital in Elgin did not have the resources. Faith was rushed by ambulance to Aberdeen, while Joan and I followed at a more leisurely pace.

The journey was not yet over. Even this large hospital in Aberdeen did not have the expertise that was required for Faith. That night she was flown down to Glasgow and put under the care of Professor Philip Caves, a man who was renowned for his abilities for Cardiac surgery. He gave to Faith the priority of all his attention, constantly by her side following his operation on her tiny heart. Philip Caves was an Irish cardiothoracic surgeon who came from Belfast. In 1972, while at Stanford University, he pioneered the use of the bioptome and transvenous endomyocardial biopsy in the early diagnosis of heart transplant rejection. It was considered the most significant advance in antirejection therapy of the time. His influence on attitudes at Glasgow's Children's Hospital in the 1970s has been described as a "whirlwind" as he operated on newborn babies who were previously considered not fit for surgery. We were privileged that this gifted surgeon was caring for our Faith in this difficult time. Indeed she was one of these new born babies who would not be considered fit for surgery if it was not for the availability of Philip Caves. The operation was noted to have been a great success, but still the journey was not complete.

Meanwhile, Joan was still in hospital in Aberdeen where I visited each day. Before going to visit Joan I made it a practice to meet with the nurses on duty to check if there was any update and we continued to cling to hope. Whatever may happen our faith in God for baby Faith was important. Timing was crucial, the first three days were important in such a situation with a new born baby. However, the time came when the news was not so good. The staff explained that though the operation was a success it was subsequently discovered that there was another fault in the heart not previously detected. They had a limited amount of time to work on this second defect, time they did not have, and sadly this battle for life for Faith had now come to an end. It was ironic that just a year later Professor Philip Caves was to die of a heart attack whilst playing squash at the young age of 38. Amongst colleagues, Professor Caves was thought to have been the most likely surgeon to have started the UK's first heart transplant program had he lived, but it was not to be. For our family at least his name lives on in our hearts.

Joan was in a single side room off the ward which gave a measure of privacy. I walked along the corridor towards the room wondering just what I could say. I had no idea, but knew I needed to say something. Joan was reading her bible as I arrived. I had not shared the sad news yet when she directed me to what she had just read from Romans chapter 8 verse 18 which says "I consider that our present sufferings are not worth comparing with the glory that will be revealed in us." I hesitated for a moment and then started to say that I had something to say. I did not need to say any more, she knew. It was an emotional time for both of us, as one would expect, times of tears as the depth of it all began to sink in. Yet there was a sense that God was with us and supporting us even though we could not understand what we were experiencing. We knew we could not have found a way through if there was not a God who would keep His promise to be with us every step of the way in whatever experience we may suffer.

There was no possibility of hiding away from public scrutiny. A baby being flown out from the hospital by helicopter and subsequently dying was seen as a human interest story for the media. Added to that the media revealed that this was a world first that such an operation was carried out on a new born baby. It was going to be headline news in the national press. They had a story they wanted to tell the world and questions to ask. Even more important I was beginning to recognise that I needed to listen to God who had an even greater interest in our human story.

The funeral was arranged. The Funeral Directors had sensitively placed Faith's coffin in the back of an estate car rather than a hearse. Faith's coffin was so small that it was possible for her to be carried to the grave side by one Funeral Director. In a spiritual sense I knew that even with a small amount of faith we have a God who can carry us, He is the only one that can carry us through the experiences of life. There was more to come.

Following the funeral of Faith our journey continued. We drove down to Bradford in West Yorkshire where my dad was having an exploratory operation in the Bradford Royal Infirmary, a large teaching hospital. I remember visiting the hospital with my mum and meeting with the consultant who explained that my dad had cancer and, in his words, dad had just a couple of months left to live. In reality it turned out to be only 4 weeks. Dad had said that whatever the diagnosis may be he wanted to be told the result, and mum had agreed to tell him.

However, in the midst of her distress she could not bring herself to say the words. So it was left to myself to explain to dad and let him know what the consultant had said. Dad had sufficient medical knowledge to know that as it had now affected his liver the prognosis could never be good. Dad accepted the news well, in fact he dealt with it far better when it was no longer the "unknown" and seemed to be emboldened as he witnessed to his faith in those final days. He knew he was ready to meet his Lord when the time should arrive.

In the 4 weeks that followed things were happening which I could not fully understand. Questions were being asked which I did not feel that I was adequately prepared to answer. They appeared to be pastoral questions within the family. I was the youngest of 6 siblings, surely it should be the eldest in the family who should be answering these kinds of questions. I did not feel I had the answers, yet the questions still kept coming. I guess I must have been a bit slow in understanding what was really happening. Eventually it dawned on me that nobody was asking these questions because of my status in the family nor because of my personal knowledge. They were asking because of God. They were asking because they had seen what God had done to bring us through an extremely traumatic experience. It seemed that this was the last time that I could raise any objections to God's call. It now seemed clear that God was not asking about my ability but my availability. Finally I gave the answer God was calling for. "Yes Lord, I am available, use me as you see fit". During my ministry over the past 41 years I have discovered so often that my own ability is not what counts. So often I would knock on a door assuming that I would meet a particular type of situation, but went away having discovered the need was completely different. How I planned to deal with it was therefore not appropriate, I needed to say every time "Lord, you know best, you be my guide".

It was just a year left before I was due to leave the RAF. I needed to address what God desired as I applied for a three year course at the Bible Training Institute and later followed that up by applying to the Baptist college which was also in Glasgow.

A question that has been posed to me was why a Baptist ministry when God has been working with me in a Methodist church? I would say that a lot of that stems from my reading of the scriptures where I was finding so much was indicating that Baptism was meant to be "Believers Baptism" and not "Infant Baptism". I recall speaking with the Minister of the church I attended. I wanted to be honest with him and not hold back on what I was now believing to be biblical. He commended that I should go with how I felt the Lord was speaking to me. He also said he was still willing to support me as a Local Preacher even though this was not traditional Methodist teaching. So I continued to preach having gone through Believers Baptism whilst respecting the position of the church. However, when I sensed a call into full time Ministry I knew that I would then need to make a denominational decision. It is one thing to fellowship with those of a different view on Baptism, but as a Minister I would be expected to perform the Baptism that is the norm of the denomination I was in. As such it seemed to me to be more appropriate to be a Baptist Minister rather than a Methodist Minister.

The final step of my journey of faith has arrived. Like Samuel in the Old Testament I had discovered not only who was calling me, but also what my response needs to be. "Speak Lord, for your servant is hearing!"

Chapter 3
Assurance of a call

Being confident of a call into ministry is important for every Minister. The vast majority of the churches where I have served have been very supportive though for all of us there can be exceptions. Life will not always go plain sailing, much as we might like it to be, but when you have no doubt about the call that God has given then you can move forward in faith. As you have seen from the previous chapter I had been very slow in my response to the call but looking back I know without a shadow of doubt that God had certainly been leading me, and the same God would guide me into what may lie ahead even in the difficult times. When times have been difficult I have often been reminded of the words of David, the Psalmist, who declared "I will bless the Lord at all times, His praise shall continually be in my mouth" (Psalm 34 verse 1) David was experiencing a very difficult time as he wrote those words, so how could he make such a bold statement? David would say despite all of that he had tasted and seen that the Lord is good (Psalm 34 verse 8). He had tasted and seen the goodness of his God. Not everyone will agree with a Minister, for whatever reason. Sometimes that may be for good reason. In humility we must always recognise that we do not have all the answers and we need to listen and seek to work in partnership with all seeking to further the gospel.

However, there are times when the Minister may have to face false accusations. In such times as this one has to hope that those sharing in Church leadership will take their responsibilities seriously. Yet if the leadership laughs and sees it as a joke that the Minister is said to be at fault even if he was not present at the time that's being referred to then that is worrying for the future of a local church. Indeed the more that happens the greater the risk that the Minister will indeed make real mistakes due to the pressure being felt. Likewise, if any assume they have a right to insist that a Minister should minister in a way that contravenes the advice of a medical Doctor when it is possible to effectively minister in other ways then I would have deep concerns for the future of such a church. It is possible to preach from any position, for example, there is no reason a Minister cannot preach from any position and that it must be from a pulpit when a Doctor advises that it is not appropriate medically. Finally, in that last example if prior to a call a Minister preaches four times without the use of a pulpit and the church votes to call him or her then one must assume that he was audible for those who voted even if it is not from the pulpit. If the Minister can not be heard it is impossible to determine if the church believes the preaching is sound. As such, no church that takes a call seriously would call a Minister if he cannot be heard. Could these examples happen for real? Yes they could, it was my experience though only in one place. When these matters were discussed it was said that I had shown before accepting the call where I would be preaching the response was "Yes, but we thought we would get you to change after arriving". For both minister and church there needs to be an honest presentation of where we see things at the time, failing to do that does not demonstrate the respect we should have for the process of issuing a call to the local church.

In that situation I moved forward knowing that it was Gods calling into ministry. I struggled to know what was the right decision to make at first. I do not like to run away from issues yet the message from the Doctor was clear as he addressed a matter that related to a past injury. If I can preach without looking down from the pulpit I can hope for many years of ministry ahead, but if I was only allowed to preach from a pulpit then the time would come when I would start to fall over. The result would be the end of my ministry completely, so what was I to do when I was so sure of God's call into ministry. I moved to another church that did understand the process of calling in a local church, and they have been very supportive prayerfully in all that followed. When I announced to the church that I would be moving on I had no idea where I was going, but it was something that I knew I had to do as a step of faith. God had demonstrated already that He wanted me to be available to minister and I believed that God would guide in what lay ahead at this time. What lies before me is a journey where I continue to believe that God has shown to me that ministry has come to me as a Divine calling. I must add that this is not necessarily determined by a position in any specific church. Indeed my assurance has come to me in the most unlikely of places and sources.

There was a period in which I was conducting a more itinerant ministry. There was no regular set income and so I would look to other ways to ensure there was financial support. One of those ways was to take up an employment delivering pizzas in Edinburgh. I quickly needed to get a good grasp of the layout of the streets. It was essential to be able to make deliveries as quickly as possible in order that the customers could get their food as hot as one would desire it to be. From a business perspective it is important that the customer is satisfied. There was a variety of backgrounds I found in regard to those customers as the deliveries were being made and as such a variety of expectations. So for one house I went to I rang the bell at the front door. Eventually a lady called me from the back door. Having handed over the purchases and the money was paid the lady then said that I was to remember when I come again that I was always to go to the back door, never the front door. The front door was only meant for the likes of the Doctor or the Minister, but certainly not for the pizza deliveries. Knowing I was, indeed, a Minister I guess that it was a time to learn humility, but there were some positive situations that encouraged me in my long term ministry hopes.

Edinburgh is a really wonderful city in so many ways, beautiful, historic, full of interesting shops and restaurants and one of the greatest cultural centres on Earth but the outskirts of the city, and some of the central bits too, have really major problems. Some of the large housing schemes on the outskirts of Edinburgh can have some 'interesting' characters residing in them who you wouldn't necessarily like to meet on a dark night, or during the day for that matter. Areas with some of the rougher schemes include Wester Hailes and Oxgangs. Those are areas that I often would visit and I recall that Wester Hailes was a sprawling concrete jungle on the city's Western flank. Often I would find myself on the doorstep of a customer talking about some of the concerns they were experiencing. I would quietly listen to them as they poured their heart out, using me as a sounding board. Occasionally I would respond to questions that they raised. I could not prolong the visit too much as there was another order waiting for me when I got back to the shop, but I responded in a manner that was appropriate to the situation. Why were they opening up their hearts to me? I was just the pizza delivery man at this time. I had no other official role, yet here they were speaking with me as if I was their Pastor. That was a puzzle to me at the time. However, this was later to become a source of great encouragement to me. The call that God had given to me was not merely down to how I was dressed or what title society may bestow upon me. It was not about any human status. It was more important for people to see a Pastoral heart. Above everything it has to be God's call or it is nothing at all. This was the essence of what was happening on these dark evenings as young people were searching for words that would bring light into the darkness of their lives. As I would drive back I would not only reflect on the discussions we had together but also the steps that had confirmed my call into the Ministry. Once again I was reminded of the verse that God repeatedly gave to me from 1 Peter chapter 5. "Feed the flock of God which is among you, taking the oversight thereof, not by constraint, but willingly; not for filthy lucre, but of a ready mind". My call was not about my position, and never should be, but it must always be about being available as God opens up the opportunities.

Let me now mention a young lady called Karen (not her real name) who lived in another part of Edinburgh. Karen was a very attractive lady, so attractive that she worked as a model though sadly by the time I met her one would never realise this was her background. In just one moment all of this changed, literally in a flash all of this was gone. She had met her future husband when she was just 16 and fell pregnant a year later. Her husband who was eight years her senior was extremely violent and stopped her from seeing her family and friends. He was deeply involved in the worst part of society as a drug dealer. It did not help that as an attractive model she would often gain the attention of men who admired her and as the jealousy increased so did the violence. There is never any excuse for abusive behaviour however in any relationship.

She eventually left him but a court order insisting he stay away from his former partner was to prove ineffective and on the 13th of February, 1991, her life was changed forever when the man that her husband hired to throw acid into his ex-wife's face carried out this very cruel attack while he sat and watched from a car nearby. He had decided that if he could not have Karen then no other man would. She was left horribly disfigured in this assault and left blind by a man paid £3000 to hurl a pint of sulphuric acid in her face. Her two young sons were also injured in the attack though unlike Karen they did not lose their sight. Even the children did not escape the wrath of their father.

At the age of 26 she had a tremendous future potentially to look forward to, but in one moment that was all gone due to one man's bitter jealousy. Karen was a customer that often rang up for a delivery, which was not surprising as she sought ways to feed her family with her sight now gone. With her regular requests for deliveries we often got to meet. She said on one occasion: "I am blind and still I am trying to bring up my two children despite my disabilities. I had to tie a bell to the youngest of my children when he was small so I could tell where he was. I would do anything to ensure their safety." She clearly cared very much for her young family and wanted the best for them. Despite the tragic situation placed upon her she still kept her sense of humour, making light of her injuries as she spoke of how she wondered if anyone would fancy a "blind date".

Throughout my ministry I have recognised myself as the Pastor of a specific local church, but I also believe it's equally important to be a Minister in the surrounding community. Community involvement is something that I have always considered to be crucial. That is the place where our preaching on the love of God begins to make practical sense. It is in that way that we discover the opportunity of developing the links that need to be there if we want to share Gods love on the long term. Our relationships in our community are so important. Meeting with Karen reinforced that view for myself. Outside of the walls of the church is a world that is full of people who have great needs, and those needs can only be met by a great Christ. That is the message that a Minister of the gospel is commissioned to bring to the world. How can we speak of the love of God if we cannot be prepared to be with the people when they are needing to know God's love is touching them. As Paul might have said "My God can meet all your needs through Christ Jesus." (paraphrased from Philippians chapter 4 verse 19)

Chapter 4

Matches and Dispatches

Matches and dispatches! Funerals and marriages are perhaps an area that many people assume is the primary task of the Minister. I don't know that I would agree with that. There are a wide number of matters that need to be focused on as a Minister seeks to direct people on the path of discovering the fullness of an abundant life. However, as that is the view of some people let's look at the realm of matches and dispatches, beginning with funerals. From my own experience I would say that one must be prepared for the unexpected. Things will not necessarily go to plan.

Part 1
Dispatches

I recall as a student the college arranged for us to visit a local crematorium. We were shown everything that was possible for us to see, including the ovens where the cremations would take place. The staff wanted us to see everything in order that we could reassure any families that we may meet that their loved ones were looked after respectfully. They explained all about the procedures that had to be carried through in the process of a cremation, from the arrival of the body through to the presenting of the ashes. All of these things are important, but one other thing that I was to see was to have a lasting impression upon me. I picked up a hymn book at random and turned to the page to where the twenty third psalm could be found, "The Lords my Shepherd". It was one of the few pages that had the marks of an extremely tear stained page. This was a hymn that was so often used at a funeral, but the page revealed the depth of feelings that would have been experienced by the mourners. Why was it that this sight left the most lasting image for me as I sought the care needed to be given at these times? Here was the reminder of the emotional feelings of the people, a reminder of how fragile are the hearts of the people, and how crucial it is for us to care for the people when they are at the depth of their fragile life. The badly tear stained pages reveal the symptoms of hearts torn apart. Beyond the procedures we must never forget the people themselves.

Meeting with one bereaved family the daughters made what seemed like a reasonable request to me. They asked if their dad's brother could say a few words in the service. It is reasonable to assume that the brother of the deceased would be wanting to say some positive things about the deceased. I invited the brother to come forward during the service to say a few words and waited to hear the kind of words that would fit with my understanding of a tribute. It was not going to be. He began by speaking of the wonderful things that **he** had done for the deceased, so it was a tribute more to himself. He then went on to publicly denounce the widow. I should have realised that there was something inappropriate about to be said when he started to use the words "this may not be appropriate to say here but …." It was not appropriate and he clearly knew it was not appropriate when he used those opening words. The funeral service is a time to bring comfort and nothing else. Indeed once something is said it can never be taken back, it is out there in the public. What has been heard can never be unheard. Things seemed to get worse as others in the congregation at the crematorium began to shout out their response. Everything was quickly moving away from what should be happening. It was at this point that I recalled the deceased once confiding in me that there was some in his family who would probably even manage to start an argument at his funeral. Sadly, it appeared that he had got that right and I had failed to take this into account.

How does one deal with such a catastrophe? As I said earlier, words uttered cannot be taken back. It's all out there. At this stage my guess is that there is no perfect answer, but this is how I responded. I knew that one of the daughters was also due to say a few words as well. I wanted to turn the focus of attention in a new direction. I physically turned away from looking at the brother, he was wanting attention and he needed to see that I had a more important focus than he was offering, and then invited the daughter to come forward. I put my arm around the daughter to symbolically indicate my support and encouragement for her and her mother. I then reminded the folks about what is appropriate in the context of a funeral service when invited to give a tribute to the deceased.

The daughter and myself then stood together as she brought a more appropriate tribute to her father. This was a new experience for me and I honestly did not have a clue how to deal with it, but was so pleased that it seemed to be the correct answer to the dilemma as some form of sanity began to return to the assembly. These are the kind of times when we do not have the opportunity to consult with others, we have to quickly learn on the job. In ministry this may often happen, but how much better if we can learn the principles from someone who has gone before us.

Speaking with the brother later he said that whatever he said about the widow he would always be there for his nieces, he would give them whatever support that they needed. I looked him in the face as I asked him how he expected them to respond to such an offer after he had publicly denounced their mother at the funeral of their father. It was a time when they needed to feel love and nothing else. He looked at me and fell silent. He had no answer.

It is worth noting that for some people this is the only time that they have the opportunity to hear themselves speaking out. It is the only time they feel people might listen to them and so they voice whatever they wish without much thought. However, the officiating Minister and nobody else is the one that is responsible for what is said and how the service is conducted. If it goes wrong he is the one to blame. When I reflect on my own experience I would say that if there is any doubt about what would be contained in those "few words" that would be uttered, then the Minister should exercise his responsibility by asking what his or her intentions are. Having done that the Minister needs to consult with the family as to how a more fitting tribute to the deceased can then be given. Allowing a repeat of the experience that I have just detailed will never be helpful for the bereaved family.

I am conscious it could have been worse. It was about this time, not too far away, that another funeral which I was not present at also gathered by a graveside. None of those working on that funeral were aware of a family feud that existed. Hidden amongst their clothing some of the family were armed with machetes. Imagine the shock that the Funeral Directors and the person officiating must have had as these weapons were revealed by the different family factions that faced each other. It should not be a surprise that those involved in that funeral were in great need of counselling, and I understand that it was indeed given to them. It is fortunate that such situations do not arise every day though one needs to be aware that bereaved families are going through a very stressful time and stress may often bring out the worst in people. They are in need of people who know how to lighten the stress load in the situation.

It was an interesting day when the Funeral Director phoned and asked if I would conduct a funeral for a lady called Mrs Mary Fraser. I agreed to do so and made telephone contact with the family. However, before I managed to visit I had a subsequent call from the same Funeral Director asking if I would carry out a funeral for a lady called Mrs Mary Fraser. I reminded him that I had already agreed to conduct the funeral, to which he said this is another Mary Fraser. I realised that this was going to be tricky. Funerals for two ladies with the same name as each other, died within minutes of each other, lived a street away from each other, both funerals would be on the same day, one in the morning and the other in the afternoon. All conducted by the same minister and the same Funeral Directors. I knew I needed to be careful. I visited the first family and they explained that though her name was Mary everyone knew her as May. I breathed a sigh of relief, there was a difference. However, when I visited the second family I heard the same sentence, her name is Mary but everyone knew her as May. Such a situation requires a minister to be sure that everything is correct. My notes were checked and double checked in the hope that all was correct.

From my perspective the process of bringing comfort must begin from the first meeting that I have with the bereaved family. That first meeting has to be more than just an opportunity of gathering information, though to some degree that is required.

My last ministry in Scotland I was working with the church and in the community for 20 years and therefore I became well known in the community. So unlike most of my Baptist colleagues I was usually officiating at three funerals in a week. We each need to discover how we find that balance within our perspective abilities, but I strongly believe that we cannot preach about the love of God if we are not prepared to be with the people who are in need of discovering God's love. I know names are easily forgotten, and should not be, so I will make sure the names are always written down. But I try to keep the writing to a minimum. I want to interact with the people and do not wish to allow the book to come between me and the family. However, bearing in mind what I have said already about the risk of confusion we need to be really sure of how much we can do without the taking of notes. However we may approach this time the needs of the family must always come first.

We do not bring much comfort to the family if we are seen to be critical, particularly in relation to their loved one, so I like to discover something positive about the deceased without being dishonest. Those listening will soon know if the narrative fits with the person being talked about. Sometimes such a process may be far from easy, but it needs to be worked on. On one occasion I had to go back to his primary school years before I discovered something more positive in his life, but it was there.

This is a ministry for all ages. Death is no respecter of age. I have conducted funerals for people in excess of 100, one who was 105 years old. Yet there were also young people in their 20's and 30's, even a few teenagers. Whatever the age, whatever the cause of death, all families need to know someone cares about them and the one they love.

One more thing. What about the Minister? The Minister gleans all the information that is required, stands in front of the congregation, and leads a service of comfort that is personally relevant for this particular family rather than a set service that can be slotted in for any given family. However, a question that has often come to my mind is what happens if the Minister should fall ill in the middle of the service. At that point there does not appear to be any stand by Minister to immediately take over. I never knew the answer till a day when I began a cremation service in Wolverhampton. I was ready, I was prepared, when suddenly I realised I was not well. It must have been obvious to those looking on as one of the family posed the question to me enquiring whether I was well. I could not hide the reality, and the last thing I remember was that I replied no, and then collapsed.

I was taken into the vestry and a nurse who was waiting for another funeral was brought in to assist till an ambulance arrived. Later I was to find it amusing when arriving at the hospital and hearing the Paramedic explain that "Reverend Magee was conducting his funeral". I wondered how I could manage such a miracle as to conduct my own funeral. That leads us to ask, what was happening at the crematorium at this time?

The Funeral Director did well as he immediately took control. He had a book of prayers and readings in his inside pocket so he could ensure that some form of a service could continue. He did not have the personal details of the deceased, so that would limit how he could make it personal for this family. To cover that he asked if one of the family could say something about their loved one. I must commend him for taking responsibility in this way, but what if no member of the family felt able to speak in this way. Perhaps there needs to be some thought given to the Minister and Funeral Director consulting on this prior to the service.

For a Christian death is not the end of the journey of life, but is the beginning of a new chapter in the story of life. Jesus sought to bring comfort to his disciples as he spoke of what lay ahead. He spoke of how God was preparing a mansion for them, preparing for them the best that could be given. There is the hope that we can know. I recall visiting a lady in a Nursing Home who was over one hundred years old and was approaching the end of her earthly life. As it turned out I discovered there were two people in the same position in that same home. I spoke with the Matron of the home who sadly spoke of the two and how one appeared to be so much more at peace than the other. She then said how she had been with so many of her residents who were approaching their last breath, and so often she had observed how the person of faith would face these moments far better than the others. I may have been the minister but the matron was the one who gave the reason for this as she said the person of faith had confidence of where they are going.

What does the bible say reference death, our loss and our need of comfort? Loss is an inevitable part of life. Losing somebody close to you, like a family member or a dear friend, can be tough and overwhelming. Fortunately, you're never alone in dealing with grief and loss. God is right there with you, even in the darkest of hours. The Bible reminds us that there's a time for everything and that grief isn't forever. As written in Ecclesiastes chapter 3 verses 1-4:

"There is a time for everything, and a season for every activity under the heavens: a time to be born and a time to die, a time to plant and a time to uproot, a time to kill and a time to heal, a time to tear down and a time to build, a time to weep and a time to laugh, a time to mourn and a time to dance,"

There's never just one "season" in life. Today might be time to mourn, but you won't mourn forever. Eventually, you'll heal, and the time to laugh will come again.

Another verse that reminds us that grief isn't forever is Luke chapter 6 verse 21: *"Blessed are you who hunger now, for you will be satisfied. Blessed are you who weep now, for you will laugh."* Jesus promised that people who are sad today won't stay that way forever. There will be happier times in the future.

The Bible also reminds us that God is always with us and that He is close to brokenhearted people, as written in Psalm 34 verse 18: *"The Lord is close to the brokenhearted and saves those who are crushed in spirit."*

Part 2
Matches

Weddings! These are the joyful moments of ministry. It is a time of celebration when couples want to cement their relationship together by declaring their love for each other in a ceremony that recognises the role of God in their lives. I believe that Jesus also saw these times as being important too. It is at the wedding feast at Canaan that we find the first record of a miracle of Jesus, the turning of water into wine. This record seems to emphasise how important relationships are to our Lord that this wedding feast was the marker of the first miracle that Jesus performed. Even today, when the Lord Jesus has been invited into a relationship then miracles can still happen as they seek to find a way through the struggles of life. All relationships need to be worked on, and how much better it would be to know that there is a God who cares about how we can progress through those struggles of life. In that sense it is right and proper to see a Christian marriage as one in which there is a partnership of three people, the Bride, the Groom, and God.

I should say that my ministerial involvement officiating in weddings has been in Scotland where the laws relating to weddings are different to England where I currently minister. However, for the purposes of writing here I do not intend to be spending time referring to the legal elements of weddings, but sharing something of the joy filled experiences that are the essence of taking part in the weddings. It is the hope that this joy is something that will continue of course. Personally I do find it particularly sad when a marriage that I have officiated in should fail. Rightly or wrongly I feel that I have perhaps let the couple down. Yet I need to remind myself that just as a parent may raise a child and when they reach an adult age they must let them go, in the same manner the Minister has to let the couple go as they learn the lessons of life together. However, a responsible Minister does not agree on the phone to perform a wedding, but rather agrees to meet with them both and together discern if this is a right path to take with this couple. It is important to talk through all the issues together first and then to agree to officiate. Having said that we can never forget that these are extremely emotional times as the tears will emerge, even with the Grooms. I say that not as a criticism, the tears are an indication that this is a person who recognises that there is something important that is taking place here, something they are serious about as they make their commitment to each other. (This is a good moment to be reminded that on a practical note paper handkerchiefs need to be ready and available for any who might need them.)

In Scotland Christian weddings can take place in any part of the country. It is the Minister present, not the venue, that determines whether the wedding can legally take place, the Minister is the one who is licensed and not the venue. However, whatever the venue may be, I do make it clear that I am there as a representative of the Christian faith and that will, therefore, be reflected in the form of wedding service that is performed.

The variety of venues is something that delights me as it often brings a reflection on what are the central interests of the couple and maybe what has brought them both together and not just some romantic sentiment.

One couple had a deep interest in quad bikes. Every moment of their leisure time would be spent enjoying their common interest as they raced around the track. This was the heart of their life. This was what had brought them together and this is where they wanted to declare their undying love for each other. So here we gathered out in the open in a Scottish field among the quad bikes and the bikers. All their friends were there to support them. All wanted to be part of this special day just as they had spent so many occasions in this same place. Why not make this the venue where they can celebrate the most important decision of their lives? Now it was not just about the love of a sport but also the love of each other as two families come together as one. They shared their vows in this venue, sealed with a kiss and the signing of the marriage schedule.

The variety of venues also opened the opportunity of meeting a variety of interesting characters. I recall a castle where I performed a number of weddings. The first time I officiated at the castle I arrived early for the rehearsal to ensure there were no problems. I soon discovered that the laird of the castle was a bit eccentric. As we were so early he offered to show me around the castle. At the end of the tour he asked if I would like to see his private quarters. I decided to humour him and agreed. As we came into the living room he said "Now here is something that would interest you". Laid out in the living room was his coffin which he had personally made and even decorated. It was important to him that he personally had his own involvement in what will be the last event of his earthly life. He said that the only problem was that he had to keep changing his dates each year.

It was at the same castle that I made another discovery when it came to health and safety. The chapel in the castle had no electric lighting. It was still the same as it had been throughout the centuries. The room was lit by candle light, which for some would add to the magic of romance but I fear that one day could result in a terrible accident. Due to the form of lighting as one came through the door it was difficult to see adequately. Eventually the eyes would adjust to the lighting, but that does not help when you first enter the room particularly as there was a step down as soon as you came through the door. My advice to the couple was always to ensure that there were two stewards at the door armed with torches. The last thing they would want is to see granny being rushed to the hospital following a fall at the wedding.

Yet within this setting came an illustration that's always important in a wedding message as a couple begin their lives together. Life will often seem dark as we work our way through, but it will work out better if we find a light to guide us through, a means of avoiding the possibility of tripping up on the way. We all need a guide, and as a Christian I believe that the best guide is Jesus, the one who is described as being "the light of the world".

There can also be elements of humour taking place. I recall the time when I was reading from 1 Corinthians chapter 13 during one wedding. It is a well known chapter that speaks of love. As I was reading I noticed that the best man was waving the order of service behind the bride. I did not know what it was all about but was determined that I would not allow this to be a distraction as I read the words of love. It was a very hot summer day and unbeknownst to me a bee was attracted to the bride's hair lacquer. As I completed the chapter of love, the Best Man stamped on the floor and said loudly "Its dead!". The irony is clear that in the midst of words of love came the declaration that it is dead!

We live in an age when a word about mobile telephones needs to be mentioned. There was a time when telephones were left at home or in the office. We left the respective buildings wanting to escape the calls, but not anymore. People take their phones with them. To be fair, there was only one time that a telephone was heard at a wedding I officiated at, and the phone belonged to the groom. Being dressed in his kilt he struggled with embarrassment to locate his phone inside his sporran. It may have only happened one time, but I would still say that prior to any wedding the congregation must be advised about their phones.

As a Baptist it will not surprise you that I mention **Baptism** in the context of a section that refers to "matches". I titled this chapter as "Matches and dispatches", a slight misquote from "Hatches, Matches and Dispatches". For us Baptism is something more than the hatches that some traditions will think relates to baptism. As Baptists we believe in "Believers Baptism", something that relates to a person making a commitment that is not possible for a baby to do. For me this is the highlight of the joy of "matches" as people make a declaration of faith declaring an eternal commitment of a relationship with Jesus. It is not something that is age related but faith related. It could be someone who is a teenager, for example, if they are expressing their own personal faith. In like manner it may not necessarily be a young person.

During my first ministry it was a joy to see so many young people seeking to be baptised as believers. At one stage we were having monthly baptismal services, which was very encouraging for us all in a small church. There was a real movement of the spirit in these young lives. Indeed the growth of young people in their 20's was so dramatic that very quickly my wife and I were soon among the older members of the church, and we were only in our 30's. I remember visiting the mother of one of the candidates. She had a stroke 7 or 8 years previously which had severely affected her speech. As we talked together she became very excited. I could not understand all that she was saying but one word was clear, "baptise". Her daughter's baptism was due soon and I assumed that was what she was referring to. I reassured her that we would make sure that she got transport to attend. "No, no, no" she said, "I want to be baptised!"

I had no doubt about her faith. I had no doubt that she had made a commitment. I had no doubt that she was spiritually qualified, but due to her health was she physically able to go through what is expected of her when it comes to full immersion with Believers Baptism? Yet she was determined, in no way would she accept any form of alternative to what was happening to those of a younger generation. It was no surprise that we would later hear that some of the non Christian members of her family were concerned in case the baptism should cause her to have another stroke.

I knew I needed advice, I could not take a risk of making a mistake in any form. I had a friend who was a Professor of Forensic Science who I decided to speak with. That might seem like an extreme route to take since there were no dead bodies about. However, there were two important factors that my friend could bring into the equation. The first is that before reaching his current post he needed to be a doctor. He had the medical knowledge I was lacking in. The second is that he once served with the Baptist Missionary Society. As a Baptist he knew exactly what we mean by Believers Baptism. Bringing those 2 factors together and I had no doubt he was the man who could give me the best advice possible.

My friend had a number of important issues to raise, taking into account the number of years that had passed since the stroke took place. He said that it was important to be clear on the following points.

1. Ensure that the lady was being sensible in keeping to her medication.
2. Ensure that her blood pressure is stable at the time the baptism is planned.
3. Ensure that the water is at room temperature. Too hot or too cool would both create a risk of a shock. But keeping precisely to room temperature would take away all risks.
4. Be sure to have another person in the water with me when I baptise the lady. This would be an added factor of keeping her safe.

The advice was clear, the sensible way forward is to keep to all of these factors. To do so then there is no medical objection to a baptism taking place. His final words, from the thoughts of a Doctor, was "Jon, if you keep to this criteria then the reality is that it is no different to lowering someone into a bath, which many patients experience". Those were the words that settled everything from my perspective as we prepared for the baptism that she requested.

I remember how we gathered for a dry rehearsal. I often would have such a rehearsal so everyone knew exactly what they were doing. It was during this rehearsal that a new shock was to emerge as the lady said with her limited abilities of speech "My testimony, what about my testimony?" Up till this time I always gave a candidate the opportunity to speak of how they came to faith and they had so far agreed to do that. This time I never offered the opportunity for her to do the same due to the limitations of her speech. I did not wish her to be humiliated in this way, but she was insistent, she wanted to let everyone know why this was so important to her. She was not going to be deterred, and so we relented. What a result it was to be! It was a close community, everyone knew of how difficult it was for her to communicate in everyday conversation. On the day of the baptism, however, she stood in front of everyone and spoke in front of a packed church building. Her testimony was one that was delivered word perfect. There was not a dry eye in the building as folks from the community who had come to this special event had no doubt that something had clearly happened in this life. They had never seen the likes of this before.

Usually the baptisms took place in the church building, but 3 young people requested to be baptised in the sea for differing reasons. There were 2 baptised on one occasion and one on another occasion. Two young ladies being baptised on the south of the island had a bigger impact than any would have realised. Even I was not aware till I saw a video of the event later on. On the video it was clear that the ferry was passing behind us as the ladies were baptised. As they went into the water the ships hooter was blown as a way of the crew declaring their support. It was reported later that many of the passengers had come to the one side of the ferry to witness what was taking place.

What is the reason for people being prepared to take this action as they are fully immersed in the water? The water itself does not provide salvation, so what lies behind it all? It is a public declaration of a decision already made in our hearts and lives. When Paul spoke of baptism he spoke of it as being two pictures in words. First of all he spoke of it as being a picture of what happened to Jesus. As we go into the water, completely buried in the water, it is a picture of what happened to Jesus as he was completely buried in the tomb on that first Easter weekend. As we rise from the water it is a picture of how our Lord rose to the newness of life. In the same way it is a picture of what happened to the believer when they trusted Jesus as their Saviour and Lord. Water baptism is merely a sign of something greater.

Whilst speaking of baptism I want to speak of a couple of practical issues that arose ealy in my ministry. As I approached my first baptism it was explained to me that the church had some fishermans waders which the Minister always used when baptising, so I should do the same. Being a young minister I decided to do as I was told. On the day of the baptism I put on the waders and made my way down the steps into the water. It was at this point that I realised there was something really wrong. The waders leaked, and it soon became evident that the waders were filling up with water very quickly. No one else would have known, but I did. The waders were of no use at all. As the baptism was completed I stood at the top of the steps and waffled as much as I could till the waders were empty. The moral of the story is two fold. One, always check the equipment before using them. Secondly, there are times that we should not just do as we are told.

On another baptism there was a guest speaker from the Baptist Union with us. Rev. Eric Watson was the Superintendant at the time. The one being baptised had friends who were not usually in the church that she had invited to come along for this special service. They soon relaxed in the fellowship, stretched out their legs, and discovered a suitable foot rest under the pews in front of them. It was not till later that they made the discovery that the "foot rest" was actually an electric heater. As they left one of them said to Eric "I thought that churches were meant to save soles". Eric kept a serious look as he replied "Thats correct, we are indeed here for the saving of souls." The visitor then explained that he had just lost his (on the heater). I am not sure that Eric understood what was being said, but we all need to understand that our visitors need guidance as to how things maybe as they come into the church. On a spiritual note, we need to come to realise and respond to the call of the Saviour as Jesus saves our soul before we consider baptism.

Baptism is an important event in the believer's walk with Jesus Christ that symbolizes new life with the symbolic use of water. The Greek root word Baptizo means to plunge, immerse, sink; hence to wash, to be immersed. The Bible talks about water immersion baptism, in which a believer makes a public confession of their faith. The Bible verses about baptism guide us to the meaning of baptism for repentance, declaration of faith, and new life in Jesus Christ. Jesus's baptism led the way for us as an example of this important event. John the Baptist, who baptised Jesus, taught that the immersion into the water was symbolic of a turning from sin and raising to new life in Jesus Christ. The act of water baptism is an outward sign of the inward change accomplished by the baptism of the Holy Spirit.

At the Ascension Jesus said "All authority in heaven and on earth has been given to me. Go therefore and make disciples of all nations, baptising them in the name of the Father and of the Son and of the Holy Spirit, teaching them to observe all that I have commanded you. And behold, I am with you always, to the end of the age." The command of Jesus at this time is clearly speaking of the importance of baptism for his disciples, but not that we are saved by baptism. At the point of baptism they are already disciples and made that important step that comes with belief. Jesus is giving a three step movement as we grow spiritually. Those 3 steps are:

1. Make disciples, leading and guiding folks to make a step of faith.
2. Mark the disciples through baptism.
3. Mature the disciples as they are taught more in matters of faith.

CHAPTER 5
Facing the elements

PART 1
Flight into the unknown

NIMROD MR2

It was the afternoon of Thursday 12th June 1986. As I drove through into Port Ellen it seemed like a normal day, yet there was something that was very different as I drove along Frederick Crescent. It was quite eerie even. It was a sight that reminded me of my past, yet a sight I never expected to ever see again. Almost hovering above the island housing was a Nimrod, which was the last aircraft I had worked on when I served as an Electronic Technician with the Royal Air Force at RAF Kinloss in Morayshire in the north east of Scotland. I was amazed at the sight. What on earth was it doing here?

The Nimrod aeroplane, with its twelve man crew, is capable of operating in a variety of roles including communications and surveillance support to ground forces; maritime reconnaissance; anti-submarine warfare and search and rescue. The Nimrod had more than enough Electronic equipment to meet these needs, indeed more electronics than most aircraft.

The Nimrod, a name which literally depicts a "mighty hunter" which aptly describes the roles it carried out, was a variant of the De Haviland Comet. It was arguably the best antisubmarine and Maritime Reconnaissance aircraft of the Cold War era. It was designed as a Royal Air Force maritime patrol aircraft, its major role being anti-submarine warfare (ASW), although it also had secondary roles in maritime surveillance, air-sea rescue and anti-surface warfare.

The development of the Nimrod patrol aircraft began in 1964 as a project to replace the Avro Shackleton. The Nimrod design was based on that of the Comet 4 civil airliner which had reached the end of its commercial life. The Nimrods were not modified Comets; rather they had taken the design of the Comet, modified it extensively, and then built a new aircraft, which became the Nimrod. The Comet's turbojet engines were replaced by Rolls-Royce Spey turbofans for better fuel efficiency, particularly at the low altitudes that were required for maritime patrol.

I reflected on each of these roles in my mind, yet continued to ask myself the question, "Why here?" There had to be a major reason and it led me to the conclusion that something was severely wrong. What could it be? Most of the roles I referred to did not fit into this scenario, but I knew there was one possibility. I checked the time and was realising what else should be happening about now. The afternoon the Logan air flight was due to arrive. It is literally a life line for the island community, it was the means of quickly getting out to Glasgow on the mainland, including keeping hospital appointments. I briefly stopped to speak with someone I knew who confirmed my worst fears. The plane had crashed into a hillside above Laphroaig on the south side of the island.

I made my way to join the other men making their way up the hill side. I had no idea what I was going to see at the top, or how I would be able to help, but as a local Minister I knew I needed to be with them and any who may have survived the crash. No Minister or local church can legitimately speak to anyone of the love of God if they are not prepared to be with the people when they are needing to see and experience God's love. Once again it is not merely about our ability but also our availability. It is in this kind of situation that one never knows what one can do or say, but just to trust God to reveal the answers as we arrive. But what has led to this situation?

Logan air Flight LC423 was a scheduled passenger flight from Glasgow Airport to the island of Islay. The handling pilot, who occupied the first pilot's position, had recently converted to flying the DHC-6 Twin Otter aircraft, and was completing a series of supervised route flights required by the airline before being given the award of full command status. A company supervisory captain, the designated commander for this flight, occupied the co-pilot's position.

The Twin Otter's engines were started at 14:38, and, at 14:44, Glasgow Airport Air Traffic Control approved taxy clearance to the holding point of runway 28. The aircraft took off from runway 28 at 14:48. The flight to Islay had now begun. At

15:10, having already started to descend, LC423 contacted Islay airport, reported an arrival time of 15:23, and requested details of the latest weather. The Islay radio operator replied that the weather details were a surface wind of 220°/05 knots, visibility 2000 metres in drizzle and cloud. LC423 acknowledged the information they were given and was asked to advise when they were overhead the aerodrome at 3600 feet, or when they were in visual contact.

The aircraft then continued to descend, on a track of about 260° towards the south side of the island, until it disappeared from radar cover at a height of 1400 feet and at a position 12 nautical miles from Islay aerodrome. From the position that the aircraft descended below radar cover it was estimated that a direct track was flown towards the southern coast of the Isle of Islay.

The flight continued at a very low level parallel to the south coast. At 15:21 the Islay radio operator transmitted further weather information which recorded that cloud conditions were similar to the previous report but that there was then heavy drizzle. LC423 acknowledged this information and reported that they were "over Port Ellen". However, in reality the aircraft was not, at that time, over Port Ellen, but was in fact turning inland at very low level over Laphroaig. From overhead Laphroaig the aircraft settled on to a north westerly heading and very shortly afterwards it crashed into rising ground that was obscured in hill fog at a height of 360 feet.

Meanwhile, down below we on the island were making our way up the hill side. I was impressed at the depth of the community spirit that was present as all worked together and made the climb. Some of the men would have used this aircraft at some point so there was something personal in all the efforts being made. Indeed I recalled being on this same aircraft not many years before as our own new born baby, Elaine, made her first journey home from the hospital. In accordance with airline policy, mother and baby sat at the back near the exit if there was a need to leave the plane quickly in an emergency, whilst I sat at the front next to a politician flying over to campaign for election. I had seen first hand something about aircraft policy to ensure the safety of its passengers. Others may have only used the Caledonian MacBrayne ferry option by sea. Some may have been thinking about family or friends who were on board. I certainly knew people who had been on the flight including one who was returning from a hospital appointment in Glasgow. Looking to one side I could see the local Doctor, Doctor Archie, struggling to manage the climb. Clearly he was vital to all possibilities in the rescue due to his medical expertise, but being very overweight he would never make it to the aircraft without some assistance. Sensing the conflict of the differing options some of the men took the initiative seeking to assist Doctor Archie. Two men came alongside him, each taking an arm as they ascended the hill side before them. When they became tired others would then do the same. My comments on Dr Archie are not intended to be offensive. (Sadly Dr Archie died many years ago). Nearly forty years later I am conscious that if it was today I would certainly not be fit enough to make the same climb up the hill either.

Eventually we reached the aircraft where it had come to rest. It was in a sorry state. During the crash, the left wing spar had broken, allowing the wing to pivot forward; the port engine propeller, still under power, penetrated the rear of the aircraft cockpit, killing the handling pilot. The supervising pilot was seriously injured, and eleven of the fourteen passengers were also sadly injured. Fortunately three of the passengers had escaped without any injuries, which was nothing short of miraculous when we consider their experiences that afternoon.

The decision of the incident inquiry was that the commander's decision to allow the handling pilot to carry out a visual approach in what was totally unsuitable meteorological conditions was most definitely a major contribution to the aircraft crash. A contributory factor was an error in navigation; in the poor weather conditions the pilots mistook Laphroaig for Port Ellen and, in doing so, turned inland about a mile too early, subsequently impacting the rising ground.

It seems to me that this whole incident illustrates an important spiritual lesson. Many may fear flying due to it being an experience they have no control over. It's something in which they need to apply complete trust in the pilot. What is often forgotten is that the pilot also needs to apply a measure of trust, not in his own human abilities but rather in the instruments that are in the aircraft designed to guide and direct them. They are all there to ensure the safety of all on board. When the instruments are neglected the risks inevitably increase. Many people may have played a vital role in our lives but they are only human, they can make mistakes. However, it is God's word that is the instrument we must place all of our trust in. All may fail but if we compare their words with God's word then there is where our confidence can be sure and certain.

In Christianity, the Bible is considered the "Word of God," and there is much to find about this topic in scripture. The Bible is called the Word of God, meaning it can be considered a direct line of communication from the Lord, divinely inspired by the authors of the respective books. As such this must always be our primary guide in discerning the direction God desires for us to take in life. I recall while I studied at the Bible Training Institute in Glasgow that the Principal, Dr Geoffrey Grogan, made it a regular practice that he would give us an A4 sheet of questions whenever we started a new series of lectures rather than a list of commentaries. It soon became apparent what his intention was. The only way we could answer the questions he had set was by reading the biblical book itself. Whatever we may find elsewhere he wisely was directing us to go to the source first of all. As we take advice from others we need to check everything with the word of God if we want to know what it is to have the best guidance in life. (For the benefit of my American readers I should explain what is meant by A4 paper. *The A4 size paper measures 8.27 x 11.69 inches, only slightly larger than the close equivalent to U.S letter size 8.5 x 11 inches.*)

Paul wrote to Timothy "All Scripture is breathed out by God and profitable for teaching, for reproof, for correction, and for training in righteousness, that the man of God may be complete, equipped for every good work." (2 Timothy chapter 3 verse 16 to 17) Well said Paul!

Part 2
Lesson in Faith from the Fishermen

The year 1986 was indeed a year of tragedy. There were a number of tragic incidents on the island in the same year, including a fishing boat that went down with all three members of the crew. It was a year never to be forgotten for all the wrong reasons. Living on an island there is a constant reminder that our lives are subject to the elements that surround us. I recall a fisherman telling me on one occasion that none of the fishermen knew how to swim. I was shocked at the time, but I was told that as they went out to sea the water was so cold that if they ended up in the water they would soon die of hypothermia. If they knew how to swim they would struggle longer and therefore suffer longer. Humanly speaking there was no hope, the only hope they had was to rely on God and trust Him. In the spiritual realm I knew that was true for us all. The fishermen were teaching me an important lesson of life which I will always be grateful for, whether they realised it or not. I need to demonstrate and live that same measure of faith in all that I do. God is the only answer to every question in my life

Chapter 6

Veterans of the past

Part 1
Destroy or rebuild?

As a Minister I have often discovered some tremendous characters in our communities. These are people who do deserve our respect in whatever we do or say. They each will bring some wonderful insights from their experiences and as we listen to them they will in their own way bring something positive to our ministries.

Jim was already retired by the time I met up with him but he had previously been the local Borough Surveyor in a neighbouring town when I lived in Fife. He was a man who had earned considerable respect locally. However, talking with him I realised there was even more to his character and had grown into his role due to his experiences in his youth. They were tough experiences but they were instrumental in shaping him into the character he had become.

Though living in Fife he was raised in the North East of Scotland and often spoke of the Doric, the language spoken in that part of Scotland and as a "loon" (boy as expressed in the

Doric) this would have been his natural tongue. There was an extensive body of literature, mostly poetry, ballads, and songs, written in Doric. In some literary works, Doric is used as the language of conversation while the rest of the work is in regular Scots or British English. A number of 20th and 21st century poets have written poetry in the Doric dialect.

However, more often he would speak of his wartime experiences, which he could never forget. He was aircrew with the Royal Air Force and regularly flew over Italy and then latterly over Germany on bombing missions. For the last three years of the Second World War the Avro Lancaster, which he flew in, was the main heavy bomber used by Bomber Command to take the war to the heart-land of Nazi Germany. With an impressive performance and excellent flying characteristics it soon established its superiority over other allied four-engined bombers that operated in Europe. The average age of the seven-man crew, which included the pilot, copilot, bombardier, navigator, radioman, and gunners, was only a mere 22 years. All young men! They endured danger and extrene discomfort and many showed great courage in continuing to fly knowing the odds against survival were high. Bomber Command suffered the highest casualty rate of any branch of the British services in World War Two. In the case of Jim it says something of the comradeship the crew shared that they never allowed the communication difficulties to prevent their gelling together as they needed to do to complete their mission. Despite his comfort in speaking the Doric Jim often spoke of the close companionship the crew knew together.

The everyday lives of most aircrew, unlike other servicemen in the war, were a unique mixture of danger and normality. At one moment the men were on a bombing raid, a few hours later they were safely at home in the pub or with family. On average the Lancasters completed only twenty-one missions before being lost. Bomber operations were extremely stressful and frequently perilous, with a random chance of death or horrific injury. Flying was physically and mentally demanding and constant concentration was needed for many hours at a time. Airmen had to not only fight the enemy, but also a hostile environment in which they might encounter many kinds of adverse weather. Occupational hazards such as the lack of oxygen, frostbite and lower pressures at high altitude meant they needed equipment to keep them warm and breathing. These problems were increased by operating in the middle of the night. The crew knew the statistics were constantly logged against them. Their time would come, they knew that every mission would bring them closer to the inevitable yet night after night the crew would begin another flight, another bombing mission. Jim was very sensitive when reflecting upon those missions. He spoke of the times he looked out, conscious of the damage their bombs had done to the people and buildings that lay below. He felt extremely guilty as he thought about this. Yet that was the task that had been allocated to him and the crew.

Jim would reflect on his last mission somewhere over Germany. They had taken a hit and instantly knew it was time to put into action all the training they had been given to endeavour to survive. If an aircraft flying over land was critically damaged, aircrew would have to bail out. Parachutes were bulky and not completely reliable, escape hatches were small and had to be located in the dark, and the aircraft might be on fire and out of control. Yet despite that they needed to attempt to evacuate the aircraft. Men were sometimes injured or killed by striking parts of the aircraft after jumping. Only 15% survived escaping from the Lancasters. Thats not many at all. Further to that landings were often very perilous. Survivors would try to evade capture as, if they were not killed by the SS, the gestapo or angry civilians, they would become prisoners of war (POWs). Jim spoke of how all these concerns were so real for them, and one of the mental strains he was later to experience was when he reflected on his friends who, unlike himself, never survived that mission. Often he would ask the question, "Why me? Why me?" At the time he could find no answer, yet he sensed that there was someone who was overseeing his life, someone with another mission of some kind for him. What could it be?

Following his capture Jim initially went with other POWs to the Dulag Luft transit camp near Frankfurt, where he was interrogated for information, knowing he was only allowed to reveal his name rank and number, and then he was transported to a permanent camp. At this point in his career he had reached the rank of Flight Sergeant. Thats a rank just senior to Sergeant and contrary to the thoughts of some who have not served "flight" does not necessarily mean he is aircrew, though he was, any more than a Wing Commander sits on the wing. It is a rank that could equally be given to someone that is ground crew. The journey between camps often offered the best chance for an escape but for Jim this was to be the end of his war. Conditions for POWs were often harsh. Food was always scarce and of such poor quality, camps were cold in the winter and often overcrowded. As the war dragged on, it became clear to every Prisoner Of War that the Third Reich's resources were being stretched thin, its attention increasingly diverted from taking care of its prisoners. They were, however, sustained by parcels of food, medicine and other comforts that were sent by the Red Cross.

Years later while I was pastorally caring for Jim as an elderly man that he disappeared from the hospital ward he was in. How on earth did he escape from a locked ward, people asked, without the security code to open the door. They clearly did not know our Jim. He was later found in the hospital cafe enjoying his coffee. He explained to me how he had watched the "guards" going in and out and memorised the codes they had used! He had not forgotten much from his POW experiences. The staff had clearly not realised his full potential, he was just an old man, but an old man who could draw on a lot from his experience of life.

However, there was something more important that he had discovered during his experiences as a prisoner. He needed to know the spiritual answers to life, and it was here of all places that he was to discover it. When given the opportunities Jim would take time to talk with the camp Padre and fellowship with others in the small chapel that was in the POW camp. He was troubled by so many of his wartime experiences and he was desperate to find the answers to life. The more he listened the more everything seemed to make sense as the Padre spoke of how he had discovered that Jesus had the answers in his own life. Without that realisation there could be no sense of direction no matter how much he tried to find it. It was in the midst of the POW camp, during the most horrendous war, that Jim knew he had to make the most important decision of his life as he trusted Jesus as his saviour and Lord. The remainder of his life he knew this was to be his "Commander in Chief", the one who would be his pilot in his journey of life. Words could never be found to express the fullness of all that meant to him. He was a Prisoner of war, yet he felt that he was a prisoner that was spiritually liberated. It was a new beginning for him as he began this new relationship with his Saviour and Lord. Captured chaplains are not considered Prisoners of War, according to the Geneva Convention, and must be returned to their home nation unless retained to minister to prisoners of war. Jim was so appreciative that this chaplain had opted to stay with the men and in so doing met his own spiritual need.

Jim knew that it was for him that Jesus said that He was preparing a mansion in heaven (John 14). Jim also reflected that in those bombing missions he had destroyed so many buildings that materially belonged to so many. As he reflected he realised there was indeed a new mission God had for him. Not one to destroy but in his new Christian faith came a mission to build for others. He determined that when the war was finished he must commit his remaining life to rebuilding. So it was that he was to eventually retire as the local Borough Surveyor, and one that all knew him as one who gave his best to helping others.

For all of us our commitment to Christ is only the beginning of our testimony. There is more to come. Not only that in the eternal realm our Lord is preparing a place for us but also that he is preparing us to be fit for what our Lord is building. In the process, there is a need for each of us as Christians to discern the personal mission in life just as it was for Jim.

Jim has now settled into the mansion prepared for him. His earthly life is over, but his relationship with Jesus is not. Jim, from myself, thank you for being prepared to share your own personal story and to be an encouragement to others on the way.

Jesus said "Do not let your hearts be troubled. You believe in God; believe also in me. My Father's house has many rooms; if that were not so, would I have told you that I am going there to prepare a place for you? And if I go and prepare a place for you, I will come back and take you to be with me that you also may be where I am. You know the way to the place where I am going." Thomas said to him, "Lord, we don't know where you are going, so how can we know the way?" Jesus answered, "I am the way and the truth and the life. No one comes to the Father except through me.

Part 2
The Wisdom of Willy

Another respected character was known in the fellowship as "Papa Willy". He was well respected as a man who had a lot of wisdom to give to the younger ones in the fellowship. One young lady spoke of how she went to see him when she was feeling low. She was hoping for comfort and encouragement, which she did find, but not in the manner that she expected. He invited her to put her coat on, he was taking her for a drive to a place that he often visited when he felt low. As they drove along the road she was puzzled, how was this going to help, the only place she knew on this road was the cemetary. As they arrived so Willy said that this was the answer to her questions. When he looked at all these graves he was reminded that his life was not as bad as these poor folks. That puts everything into a better perspective.

Chapter 7

Prison Ministry

The prisoners that are mentioned in this chapter are all genuine people I have met. However, in order that we might protect their privacy I have altered their names so that they will not be recognised.

I will never forget my first visit to Saughton Prison, otherwise known as Edinburgh prison, and the reason for my visits. I knew the prisoner, Billy, prior to his conviction and always found Billy to be a very pleasant young man always willing to give a helping hand. Needless to say I was shocked like many others when the news broke that he had been arrested. He was very open as he admitted that he was guilty of the charge. It did not seem to me that Billy had been acting in accordance with the character I had seen in him, but he was honest enough to say that he had yielded to temptation. Billy knew he had done wrong and was full of remorse. I guess for many people this would be a cut off point in terms of any continuing relationship with him, but as I see it my call into ministry was not conditional on the perfection of humanity that surrounded me. The only one perfect is our Lord who was prepared to spend time with the outcasts of society. If Jesus could do that how could I say I am too good to be tainted by associating with this young man. I agreed to meet with Billy, to talk with him, and most important to listen to him. He was a man in need.

I made contact with the prison chaplains department. Each prison has a chaplaincy team made up of at least one chaplain from each of the three main traditions. But meeting the religious needs of prisoners is only one part of the chaplain's role. By far the main part is the pastoral and spiritual care of all prisoners irrespective of faith, belief or lack of it. Chaplains form a strong link between the communities inside and outside, supporting families and caring for those most in need, helping them to discover purpose and meaning and develop the resources to live a fulfilled life. People in prison often have limited opportunities to spend time outside their cells in meaningful activities, so the services that the Chaplaincy offer can be a lifeline. This seemed to me to be the best starting point. The chaplain acted as a means of liaison between myself, the prisoner and the prison system.

H.M.P. Edinburgh is located in the west of Edinburgh, in an area now known as Stenhouse, and, although never named as such, has commonly been known as Saughton Prison from the old name for the general area. The prison is situated on the edge of a predominantly residential area, an area I knew very well having often visited the area. The day and time for my first visit was agreed and I made my way there, parked in the prison car park, and walked towards the prison entrance carrying all the documentation that was required of me. This was a new experience for me, never having been in the prison system before in any capacity. I had no idea what I would meet up with once I was inside and whether I might cope, but once more I knew that this was not about me. It is not about my ability but my availability, the rest is in the hands of the God who is more than able to meet our every need. I have found so often that it is in my weakness I can know the strength of God.

I had arrived in good time, I did not wish to disrupt the prison schedule or restrict the time required for security checking due to my being unpunctual. Once my identification had been checked and security was completely satisfied one of the staff escorted me to the prison chapel. We passed through a large number of doors. The door ahead was never unlocked till the one behind us had been locked again. It was at this point that I was glad I was not claustrophobic. For someone who suffered in this way it must be a living nightmare. Eventually we arrived at the chaplains department. I was welcomed and offered a seat whilst waiting for the prisoner who would not be escorted to the chapel till after I had arrived.

Once Billy had arrived we sat together. Someone brought a cup of coffee and biscuits for both of us. The drinking of tea or coffee is invaluable in ensuring everyone is relaxed. I have often found that this is a great aid in pastoral work irrespective of whether it is in prison or outside of prison. On this initial meeting in the prison I considered that my primary concern is to make sure that Billy knew that he was not forgotten. He was in prison, but not everyone considered that he was an outcast and his lack of freedom did not mean that Billy lacked any friends. I let him lead the conversation at first. I wanted him to know that I was interested in everything he had to say. We talked about so many things as he continued to be honest in recognising his guilt, knowing he had let so many people down. But we also spoke about spiritual things. He needed to know that there is a God who is still interested in him and cares about him irrespective of his guilt. Billy still had a sentence to complete as he paid his debt to society. Yet in tandem with that he needed to be reminded that on the eternal scale the Lord had paid his spiritual debt on the cross of Calvary. There was hope for Billy.

This was the first of a number of meetings that we would have together at the chapel in Saughton prison. It seemed to me that it was like a mission accomplished as God used this time as a life line to one who was cut off from society in so many other ways. His sentence was soon to be completed when Billy came to me with a special request. He spoke of a conversation he had before he came into prison. It was a conversation with someone who had a lot of respect throughout Scotland because of the work he did among the homeless. The man he spoke with had a lot of resources in this field and therefore it was encouraging when he made a promise that he would do all he could to help him when he needed to settle back into society. I knew the man he spoke off very well, and so Billy, the prisoner, made his request that I would speak with him to see what he could do for him. I agreed to his request.

Within the next week or two I met up with the man who gave this promise. I spoke with him about how I had heard of this promise and that Billy was now looking for assistance in finding accommodation and furniture. I did not see that there could be any problem in what I was doing, but I was wrong. As we spoke there was a pause for a few moments. Then came the response as my colleague acknowledged he would have made that promise but would not be keeping the promise. His words struck me hard as he said "Jon, you know what its like in ministry, you make promises that you never expect the person to come back to you later to claim on the promise. I said what I thought Billy wanted to hear but it was not something that I expected to have to fulfill at some point in the future". I was struck dumb in that moment. I could not see ministry in that light, and I still believe that no ministry should be carried out like that. We do not make promises with no intention of fulfilling them. Thats worse than not making a promise at all. A man's hope will rest upon a false promise.

Billy needed to know the result of the conversation I had had with my friend. It seemed to me that so much was resting upon this promise that had been given, but which would not be delivered. Billy listened in silence as I spoke, how would he react? To my surprise Billy took the news calmly and confidently declared that he accepted that my friend did not have to do anything and he was trusting that God would see him through. At the time I was new to the system, with hindsight I am now aware that there are other routes that former prisoners can take. But I still could not understand that this important promise was a failed promise. No help ever materialised from this source.

There were other factors that I was to learn when visiting the prison. There would often be times of hanging around waiting. Billy was not escorted from his cell before I had arrived in the chapel, so I needed to be patient and wait. Some of the prisoners were assigned to have a job, and one in particular was assigned to assist the chaplains. He would have had the title 'Chapel Orderly', which was a much prized role for the prisoners. This particular man was Jock. Among his various tasks Jock was to look after the likes of myself, ensuring that I was supplied with coffee and biscuits. He was not the prisoner that I was primarily there for, but I still took the time to talk with Jock as he looked after me with the coffee. We had many conversations together during this time.

Jock was a long term prisoner, sentenced to life. He told me fairly early on that he was in prison for murder. When someone has that kind of background we will usually think of him as a rough tough character. There cannot be any room in his life for sentimentality. It was at this time that extremely distressing news was coming in from outside the prison that would be quite a revelation.

It was about 8:15 in the morning on 13th March 1996, Thomas Hamilton, aged 43, was seen scraping ice off his van windscreen outside his home at Kent Road in Stirling. A fairly normal activity one might think. He left soon afterwards and drove about 5 miles north to Dunblane and soon the world would discover that the normality of that early start of the day was to become a horror story. He drove into the Dunblane Primary school car park at about 9:30 in the morning. He cut the cables on a telephone pole and then entered the school, carrying four handguns and 743 rounds of ammunition and wearing shooting earmuffs. He fired a couple of shots as he made his way to the school gym, where teacher Gwen Mayor had just taken her 29 Primary 1 students for their physical education class. Thomas Hamilton entered the gym and immediately opened fire, wounding physical education teacher Eileen Harrild and teaching assistant Mary Blake and injuring and killing several children. In total Thomas Hamilton shot dead sixteen pupils and one teacher, Gwen Mayor, and injured fifteen others before killing himself. It still remains the deadliest mass shooting to have happened in British history.

Meanwhile, in Saughton Prison the news was coming through on the radio. Hearing about each of the children being tragically killed, this rough, tough prisoner, Jock, burst into tears crying uncontrollably. This scene brought out a new insight for myself. So often we assume that we have an understanding of the nature of the people we are speaking with and fail to realise how complex human nature is. Even this tough and hardened murderer had a soft side to his character and on this day we could see him as a broken man. For me this was an important lesson in life. We should never presume we know everything about the person before us, but be prepared for the surprises to emerge.

One might wonder how we might feel if we were the victims of the criminals we were speaking off. Would we still care for them in quite the same way? That is an important question to ask. So to put things into context, what has been my experience from that perspective?

Winifred Hill, 78 years old at the time, was known to me as Aunt Winnie. She was unloading an elderly friend's shopping from the boot of her car when a man approached her and stole her handbag. There was a struggle resulting from that and the attacker knocked her to the ground, before driving off with an accomplice in a Renault Laguna. Aunt Winnie was left with serious head injuries, a broken collarbone and an injured knee as she lay on the ground across the road from the Catholic church in Haig road, Biggin hill, Kent. Sadly she was subsequently to die of these injuries.

She was a woman that was anxious to see the good side of people wherever possible and was very trusting. Whatever the feelings about what happened, it was important for us to remember the positive sides of her life. As a family we would never have thought this would happen in a place like Biggin Hill, so we were very shocked. Aunt Winnie was raised in Biggin Hill and subsequently spent her life in this peaceful part of the country. Biggin Hill sits atop an outcrop of the North Downs, now finding itself in the southern most fringes of the London borough of Bromley, tucked just inside the M25. This kind of incident is not what we would have expected here in this small corner of the garden of England . No doubt each of the family had to find their own route trying to overcome those inner emotions that we would all be experiencing. I can only speak for myself in this chapter with regard to this.

In the coming months there were many issues coming together that would have inevitably created greater stress, but they were things that had to be faced. There was the meeting with the police, of course, who were given permission to use a room in the Catholic church as an incident room, but we also met with the lawyers, the media and even a television company that was recording a "fly on the wall" documentary concerning the investigation. In addition to all of this was the continuing responsibilities that were still there for myself as the Pastor of a church in Scotland. Of course we were living in an age where technology made the combination of all this possible. With computers and the internet it was possible to carry out administration and studies anywhere in the country just as it was possible to send emails from Scotland answering queries from those working hard in the investigation that was happening in Kent.

I recall the time when we attended the Old Bailey, otherwise known as the Central Criminal Court of England and Wales, for the hearing where the defendant had pleaded guilty to Manslaughter. Prior to the hearing one of the police family liaison officers offered to give us a tour of the building. It was a most fascinating tour, I found it to be very interesting. As we walked around we saw some wonderful murals painted in various parts of the building. They were initially painted at different times of the history of the Old Bailey by various artists, bringing to life how things once used to be. During the 2nd World War these murals were damaged as a result of the bombings and the blitz of London. Following the war an artist was commissioned to repair the paintings, and as he did so he added a new dimension to it all. In each of the paintings of the different eras of history, if you looked closely enough, you could see that he had added a new character to all the paintings, himself. He also added a new painting of life in his own era, and of course he made sure he was once again added to the scene as he was in the previous paintings. It was as if he wanted to feel that he was part of all the proceedings, even here at the Old Bailey.

All who have been victims of crime will inevitably feel the pain and the anguish of it all, yet the more we become bitter the more that we effectively place ourselves into a virtual prison of life. Such action will do us more harm than good. So how can we overcome it all? I could look back and ask what my aunt would have thought about all that was happening. But here was another way of approaching things as I paint myself into the picture and say "there, but for the grace of God, go I".

What does the Bible say? I was naked and you clothed me, I was sick and you visited me, I was in prison and you came to me.' Then the righteous will answer him, saying, 'Lord, when did we see you hungry and feed you, or thirsty and give you drink? And when did we see you a stranger and welcome you, or naked and clothe you? And when did we see you sick or in prison and visit you?' And the King will answer them, 'Truly, I say to you, as you did it to one of the least of these my brothers, you did it to me.' (Matthew 25 verse 36 to 40)

CHAPTER 8

Ministry to all

"Author Jon Magee chairing a meeting with Gordon Brown, then Chancellor of the Exchequer and later Prime Minister of UK"

"Author Jon Magee with the late Helen Eadie
and Bob Eadie in the Scottish Parliament"

One thing that I have discovered is that irrespective of where folks may be on the social scale, all of us have a spiritual need. As a Minister I soon discovered that it is important to be available irrespective of who it may be or what they may even be politically. What I am about to share says more about the grace of God than it does about me.

If you visit the Scottish Parliament it is worth taking time to see the Debating Chamber. I often visited the Scottish Parliament as I met with our constituency member of the Scottish Parliament, the late Helen Eadie, MSP. On one occasion her husband, Bob, pointed to the cut out shapes in the wall of the Debating Chamber. They were the shapes of people, and as one looked at them there was a constant reminder to the politicians what their working life was meant to be about. Looking at the shapes was a reminder that they need to look out to the people as the people look in to them. The work in Parliament means nothing without that interaction, as is the case for so many of us seeking to serve in our community. Often, Helen and I worked in partnership together looking at the ways we might serve in the community together.

There are differing ways in which we can reach out to those in leadership in society. What works in one area may not work in other areas, but in time we can find what is best in our locality. When we approach an election time I have sought to find ways of engaging in what is happening. It is not a time for a minister to play at party politics, which should never happen, but it is a time to bring a spiritual input into what is happening in society. In the early days of doing this I would approach the time with an election forum. Candidates from all political persuasions would be invited to take part, as well as the community. It was the opportunity to present a whole realm of questions to those hoping to succeed in the election. As a chairman of the meeting I found it to be interesting that listening to various people attending you would think that I must have supported all the candidates. The reality is that it is not possible to vote for them all, but I took it as a compliment as it indicated that I was fair to all involved and that is so important on these occasions. However, there has to be something more to it than this.

At the beginning of the meeting I would say very clearly why the church has set up the meeting. There are two reasons that I would feel to be important. The first is that the bible exhorts Christians to pray for those in leadership. If that was so for the political leaders 2,000 years ago how much more is that the case now? The political leaders of biblical days would make our current political leaders appear to be like angels. God calls us to pray for our leaders. As followers of Christ, we need to pray for our leaders both in and out of the election season. Our political leaders need prayer, no matter who they are or which party they may belong to. And as Paul exhorted Timothy, Christians are called to pray for those "in high positions." We do this more effectively if we take every opportunity to meet with them and to hear what is being said. Secondly, I believe that Christians should act responsibly with regard to our civil responsibilities. We cannot do so without coming to listen to what they say. As we come to a close of the meeting I would pray for each of the candidates and assure them that irrespective of what the result may be we would continue to pray for them. I am sure that many of them appreciated that, and for years afterwards candidates would make contact with me and talk about specific needs. Often that would be in confidence, which needs to be respected, but though the politics may vary the trust was clearly there in the church support.

I recall following one such forum we had tea following, and the first person I spoke with was a gentleman whose colouring would indicate his ancestry was not from Europe. He spoke of his appreciation of the evening and particularly that I not only prayed for all the candidates but ended the prayer with the words "in Jesus name, amen". He said that it was the first time he had heard any in this country being prepared to recognise the importance of faith in the big decisions of life. As he spoke in that way it seemed appropriate to me to ask which church he attended. His response was to say he did not belong to any as he was a Muslim, but he had much respect for any who were true to their faith. Clearly from his position it was not offensive to come from a position of faith even if it was not his faith. What was offensive, as he saw it, was when people were afraid to speak of their faith even in their own country.

As time went by I moved on from using a forum to having what I called an "Election Dedication Service". It would be a

Christian service on a Sunday Evening immediately before the Thursday election. I made a point of contacting the incumbent MP or councillor first. When they agreed it seemed to be easier to encourage the other candidates to also accept the invitation. It was made clear that it was a Christian service and other than publicly acknowledging and introducing the candidates the only ones speaking would be myself and representatives of other churches in the community as well as a representative of the Community Council (that would be the Scottish equivalent of what is the Parish council in England). I guess the carrot for the candidates is that they are free to meet the congregation in the hall and talk with them over a cup of tea or coffee. The candidates later were to speak of it as being the highlight of their local politics as it was the first time they could relax at the end of the campaign. This was something that was particularly appreciated by candidates with little experience. One thing that did pleasantly surprise me was a candidate who came from another constituency every time we held an Election Dedication Service. She did not need to come at any time but she came because she personally found the approach was helpful for her, and there was nothing like it happening in her own area.

For me this was a crucial start in reaching out to those involved in politics without revealing which party we might be voting for. I would need to clarify that this may not work for everyone in all constituencies, but in the main it did for us. In Fife all candidates appreciated this approach as did also two constituencies I was involved with in the West Midlands. However, having tried it once in the Huntingdon constituency I admit that no candidates responded to the invitation they were given. I must add, however, that sometimes it maybe worth trying twice before assuming it will not work. Despite the previous dissapointment I felt, with the agreement of the

Deacons, that we should give it another try. This time there was a better result and very quickly there was a sharing of pastoral needs. Robert the Bruce historically declared the importance of how we must "try, try, and try again," and so must we.

In areas and times where this was successful it proved to be crucial for the long term relationship of the church and the politicians irrespective of what party they represented, including those with senior positions in the cabinet. In Scotland our constituency Member of Scottish Parliament, Helen Eadie, would often consult with me seeking to find local ears who would guide her on specific needs. Together we worked on many projects as we sought to bring answers to the needs of our people.

One particular project I recall was in relation to the Gulf War and the support of the families of the soldiers who were in Iraq. Helen and I arranged for a public meeting which was held in the church hall. The numbers gathered clearly indicated the needed support in whatever way is possible. The military does a wonderful job of supporting the immediate families, the wives and the children. I know that is true from my personal experience in the past with the military. However, wider than that will be the parents and siblings of the soldiers. Who would support them? We were living in an area that was a large recruiting centre for the Black Watch and these were soldiers who were at the heart of the fighting and as such it would reasonable to assume that we would be seeing bodies returning as well as those who would receive severe injuries.

The invasion of Iraq led to the deaths of 179 British personnel in total between March 2003 and February 2009. Some of the Britons who died were just 18 years-old. So very young Some of these soldiers came from Fife. Tony Blair told the Chilcot Inquiry into the conflict he had "deep and profound regret" about the loss of life suffered by British troops and

Iraqi civilians. I have no doubt that is true, but it is only when meeting with the families that you can really see the pain and feel its depth. Some of them have lost loved ones in the most horrific of ways, some would likewise have had the agony of seeking to support those who were injured. They had left as men of war, and returned with experiences they would rather forget, some maybe not even wanting to admit their need of support but those who loved them knew they were not the men they once knew. Emotionally what they were experiencing was tearing them apart. If we are honest we would say we do not have all the answers for any of them, but once again we need to be people who are available and willing to sit beside them at any time. Following an interview on national television it was amazing to see people offering support. I would honour that support and the people that came forward. We were a small church so on a human level that additional support was important. However, as a church may we never forget that we may be small but God is great and with him walking beside us amazing things will happen.

I spoke of that professional relationship that developed with Helen Eadie, our constituency Member of the Scottish Parliament, but I would also acknowledge the personal support I knew from Helen. Helen wrote a wonderful forward for my first published book, "From Barren Rocks to Living Stones", and I appreciated the sentiments she expressed there. She also attended the birthday celebrations of my late mothers 90th birthday and also was present at Mum's subsequent funeral. As a family we have appreciated her willingness to stand beside us in both the good times and the bad.

The opening sentence of this chapter said "One thing that I have discovered is that irrespective of where folks may be on the social scale, all of us have a spiritual need." So what about the other end of the social scale? They also have a vital need to know the light of God in their lives and it is important that we seek to respond to their every question. Some of the illustrations I will bring to you are not the people you will speak with if ministry is seen as some kind of career move. However, if we see ministry as being about a God movement then we know it is about being willing to be available to share the love of God to all we meet. A number of localities were places where I found those with addictions were soon discovered, people that society at large had little contact with. I met with many of them as I walked around the community, I even visited their homes.

In one community it was drug addiction that was the main issue where support was vitally needed. If one is working with such people there is wisdom in ensuring you are not alone, irrespective of whether you are with men or women, one never knows what may happen but that is no reason to do nothing. I have lost count of the amount of times that I would hear indications of the depth of loneliness and hopelessness many were experiencing. I would sometimes hear people saying that in the drug world they do not have real friends, just acquaintances. It was a dog eat dog world where no one could be trusted with anything. One person expressed surprise that there was a willingness to assist, saying "normal people do not want to be with the likes of us". They were seeing themselves as being the lowest of society in their community. No one would care about them. Of course, it was hard for them to understand. Many of them had never known genuine love being expressed, so often it was a word that was used to advance abuse. A real fathers love, for example, was not what they had known. So when offering help there was an assumption that something must be wanted in return. I would need to explain that friendship is not like that, it is about caring without expecting anything in return.

In time, however, there were some who felt they could confide in me about things that troubled them, things they would not say to anyone else. It took time to build that trust, but it was time that needed to be the investment in these lives. One young lady looked at me nervously as she asked if she could share a secret. She spoke of being sentenced to being in prison because she stabbed a police officer. It was something she regretted, she said, she wished it had never happened, but it did. She then looked at me nervously again as she appeared to wonder if she should have revealed this news, wondering if that would mean she would not get more pastoral support. Whether that would ever happen again is hard to say for sure. She had a young daughter, I figured that whilst her daughter was with her that was less likely though there are always risks with whatever decision one might make.

One spoke of a desire to have some help with their addiction itself. If a person needs treatment for drug addiction, they are entitled to NHS care in the same way as anyone else who has a health problem. So I agreed to take her daily to a clinic where professional assistance could be given. I did so with the proviso that her daughter came in the car with us and we would sit in the waiting room together whilst treatment was given to the mother. This was part of ensuring that there was some protection for myself, and in the waiting room other members of the public would be coming in and out. The clinician spoke with me on one occasion and thanked me for assisting. So often she tried to help addicts knowing that there was no one else to help and the addict was isolated from contact with the community other than other addicts. That meant that the temptations were constantly there, and so often her efforts were in vain. However, even with the added help it is always going to be a difficult route to take with any addict.

I knew that I always needed to keep alert in these situations. I recalled calling into a petrol station on the route to the clinic. As I paid for the fuel I caught sight of something that troubled me. The lady was admiring some small trinkets that were on display. She then did something I had never seen before. She placed the palm of her hand over one item, then lifted her hand in a manner that the salesman could not see what was being lifted in her palm. It all happened so fast, but I knew what was happening. I gave her a knowing look and she realised she had been seen. She smiled and returned the item as quickly as she had lifted it. The attendant never knew how close he was to losing an item that day. We did talk about it later and she rationalised that the shop would not suffer as it would be covered by insurance. That clearly was not how I saw it and I told her how I felt. She looked down at that point and meekly said "I am sorry".

No matter what precautions we may put in place one needs to be prepared for all kinds of situations we might walk into. I remember visiting one particular house where I was welcomed and as was often the case was offered a cup of coffee. We talked freely as we drank the coffee. All seemed to be going well when a number of associates arrived. My host disappeared and I knew I had another appointment to keep. It seemed to me that it would be rude to just go without saying something. The kitchen seemed to be the likely place to find anyone. I found more than I expected, three young people injecting drugs. It was certainly time for me to leave, which I did. Drugs may be swallowed, smoked, inhaled through the nose as a powder, or injected. When drugs are injected, their effects may occur more quickly, be stronger, or both. Injecting a drug also has more risks than other methods of use. People are exposed not only to the effects of the drug but also to problems related to injection itself The addicts I met with were predominantly those that injected. Drugs may be injected into a vein, a muscle, or under the skin. Veins in the arms are typically used for intravenous injections, but if these areas become too scarred and damaged, some people inject drugs into other veins, including those of the thigh, neck, armpit or feet. However, the addicts that I met with said they preferred not to use their arms which may more easily be seen revealing the marks of injection. Injection drug users have unique challenges because of additional social stigma, substantially increased risk for infectious diseases, the health consequences of injection drug use, and the addiction to the injection process itself. Repeatedly injecting drugs intravenously produces track marks which reveals the secret use of drugs. Track marks are lines of tiny, dark dots (needle punctures) surrounded by an area of darkened or discoloured skin. Injecting drugs under the skin causes circular scars or ulcers. The more visible the injection site, the more likely a user is going to try to cover it up with clothing, make-up, or tattoos. The ability to identify track marks is one way to detect use.

One of the three I saw in the kitchen was later to say that the first time she had seen someone injecting she thought it was like seeing a film in real life. For her it appeared as something glamorous like a Hollywood movie which motivated her to become further involved. However, despite it being seen by her as something glamorous, sadly she was to later die a young death. There was nothing glamorous in how her life ended. Once starting on the downward spiral there is so much that is going against them. Starting in the drug scene brings so much risk, but the irony is that the body can become so dependent on the drugs that failing to get a fix can result in each of the organs failing till he or she dies. Going "cold turkey" can be fatal. The more I reflect on that the more I feel that the worst offenders in all of this is the person who starts them on the drug scene, the dealers. I said that this is no easy route for a minister to work with. I did not see any big revival among these young people, but I did see young people in need of discovering the love of God in their lives.

However, there is a positive story to tell as well. Jack was one of the characters often seen on the corner of the street with the men who enjoyed more than a drink or two. I would often stop and talk with the men as I passed them when walking down the road. How much of our conversation that may have been remembered I could not be sure of, but we talked nevertheless. It was a dark Saturday night when I heard a knock at the door, and there was Jack desperately looking for answers. The question he raised as he stood at the door could have come straight from the bible. "What must I do to be saved?" He had been drinking, perhaps he felt he needed the "Dutch courage" before he uttered those words. I invited Jack into the house and talked some more as we listened to each other. Jack seemed so open that night and together we prayed. I had a question in my mind. How much is he fully understanding what is being said? As I said, he had been drinking, so when the alcohol was gone would he still be feeling the same. I took him home quite late and before we parted I said I wanted to see some signs of how genuine he was. I wanted to see him coming to the church sober the next day. The morning service came, but there was no sign of Jack. As the evening service arrived I went into the pulpit, looked out at the congregation, and there Jack sat with a relative and free from the drink. Maybe he needed to wait till the evening to be sure the effects of the alcohol were gone. There were challenges along the way but I do believe God was at work in the life of Jack on that dark Saturday night. The night was dark, but light had come into the dark life of one young man as new life dawned upon him.

In Romans chapter 15 verse 20, Paul noted one of his goals was to take the gospel to people who had yet to hear it. He said "I make it my ambition to preach the gospel, not where Christ has already been named, lest I build on someone else's foundation". It was good enough for Paul to reach to all levels of society with the gospel, so why not for us.

Chapter 9

Taking the opportunities.

Part 1
The ultimate Questions

When the opportunities arrive they need to be grasped. Let me share some of the opportunities that came unexpectedly in my own ministry. They were not engineered by myself and seemed to me to be opportunities that God provided.

John Blanchard was an internationally known Christian preacher, teacher, evangelist, apologist and author. I recalled the letter he sent to me, a letter that came completely out of the blue. He explained that during the second World War, as a young child, he lived in Guernsey in the Channel Islands. As the Germans prepared to invade the authorities arranged to evacuate the children to mainland Britain. John's brother was fostered to a Lanarkshire mining family whilst he was fostered with a crofting family in the Hebrides. Indeed it was the very island where I was ministering at the time. John explained that he was planning a trip to the island and would be with us for one night. His hope was that he could meet with any who might remember him as a young refugee child.

I went to the school where he was educated on the island and discovered the names of the children who were registered at the school at the time. As I tracked them down it was amazing how many of them could remember this blond haired child who had shared life with them some forty odd years before. He must have made a great impression on them. We arranged a meeting in the local hall, providing tea for them all. John invited his past school friends to share some of their memories, and then he did the same, filling in the gaps as he also spoke of his return to Guernsey and how he came to faith. This was a meeting that the islanders were never to forget, along with what they heard of the testimony that John spoke of.

Whilst visiting the island John did some work towards a video he was making of how he came to faith. It was a video that included the heartbreak of a child being separated from his family during the war and his time on the Hebridean island. When the video was completed many came to see this video as it was shown in numerous parts of the island. That seems like a great opportunity, but it was only the beginning of the story.

In 1987 John made contact once again, saying he was celebrating 25 years of full-time ministry and at the same time was publishing the booklet *Ultimate Questions*. He sent a copy of the booklet and told me the prices it was being sold at including bulk order prices. What stood out was the Post script he added in his own handwriting. He asked how many homes there were on the island, and if someone was to cover the costs for the books could we arrange for them to be delivered. Then he says "Just a crazy thought". I really love crazy thoughts. I told him the number of houses there were on the island and if someone covered the costs I would be delighted to arrange the delivery.

I put it to the back of my mind and forgot about it till the surprise happened. I was away at a Ministers conference and returned to hear the question "What have you ordered?" Five boxes had turned up on the doorstep! Five boxes full of books! The "crazy thought" had indeed arrived. This was our project for the year to deliver this gift to every house on the island which we endeavoured to do faithfully. As I returned home one afternoon I caught sight of Islay House. Islay House was one of Scotland's most historic grand mansion houses which has a window for every day of the year. *Islay House* is situated just outside the small village of Bridgend at the head of Loch Indaal at the centre of Islay with a dramatic outlook down the loch. I could not miss seeing this noble house. It was built for Sir Hugh Campbell of Cawdor, Nairnshire around the year 1677 and in 1985 the house was sold to Captain Thomas Friedrich of the United States Navy. He was a retired test pilot, a former US Navy fighter pilot, an aeronautical engineer and inventor (he was the Inventor of Red, A hush kit for Jet Engines), he served as personal pilot for Ugandan President Idi Amin and for one of the senior Saudi Arabian Princes. This was how he made sufficient money to purchase this grand property, Islay House, on the island that he and his wife had fallen in love with. Islay House is one of Scotland's grandest and most historic country house's, located at the centre of the Queen of the Hebrides, Islay. Set in twenty eight acres of stunning gardens and woodland overlooking Loch Indaal, Islay House possesses one of the most naturally beautiful locations in the United Kingdom. From the breathtaking views across the ornate lawns out to the sea loch to the scenic surrounding Bridgend Woods, Islay House offers everything that could be asked of a trip to Scotland. It was a grand house which was once the base for the Islay estate.

It was at this point I had one of those crazy thoughts again. We have set a vision of reaching every house on the island, but here is one house we have missed. Our vision has not been reached if we let this go. I was not convinced that we should leave out a house because it was the biggest house on Islay, the gift was for all. I prayed one of those quick telegram style prayers as I turned left and made my way along the drive, parked the car and rang the bell at the front door. I had no idea what kind of greeting I would get, but I felt that the vision needed to be honoured. It was a pleasant surprise when the door was opened by none other than Mrs Kathleen Friedrich herself, the wife of Captain Thomas Friedrich. I explained the reason for the visit and she invited me in, had coffee together, and talked. I spoke of how this booklet was his gift to the people on the island, and how he was fostered to a family who were crofters on the Islay estate. She was fascinated with the story of John, and when I mentioned that he was returning later that year she offered her own home as a place for everyone to meet for a reunion. It was amazing, the young boy who often walked past the big house on his way to school was to be the guest of honour in a house that, in his day, was not open for the ordinary folks. It was almost like a fairy story coming true, but in reality it was more than that, it was something that had sprung out of God's direction. Later that year many of us did indeed meet with John in the big house, Islay House. Tea was served, and John brought a feast of his knowledge of Christ. From one unexpected event the gospel reached many of the island homes.

In ministry our hopes and dreams come packaged in cans. We need to have a vision where we begin by saying "I can" not "I can't". How I wish I learnt that lesson earlier, what a difference I would have found in so many aspects of my life. God has so much to fill a life that is available even when we feel unable. Solomon wrote "Where there is no vision, the people perish" (Proverbs 29 verse 18). We also live in an age where vision needs to be at the heart of our ministry.

Part 2
The singer or the Song

Meanwhile, while I was ministering at Lochgelly in Fife we were looking at the visit of an American Partnership team which would be led by a retired Pastor. It is good to discover ways in which we can partner with others. Paul himself would refer in the New Testament to partners in the gospel. One difficulty this time was that the Pastor was struggling to bring a team together. One day he phoned me up to talk about his hopes for the visit. He said there was a young man in a church he used to Pastor who sings a bit and comes across to Europe at times. He said that he thought if he asked him he would come across with him to sing in the church. He said "I don't know if you have heard of him, his name is George Hamilton IV." Yes, I knew about him. George was an American country musician. He began performing in the late 1950s as a young teen idol, switching to Country music in the early 1960's. In the 1970s, George Hamilton IV was the first American country singer to have his own British TV series on BBC. In the 1980s, Hamilton appeared with Billy Graham on Ministry Tours throughout the United States and Canada, including the UK tour "Mission England". There must be very few people who had not heard of him. Would a man with such a high profile agree to come to our small church? Who knows, but one thing is for sure, he would never come if he was not invited.

Yes, George did agree to come and it looked like the team was coming together at last. We were looking forward to all the possibilities of what lay ahead. What could go wrong? It soon seemed as if everything could go wrong. A few weeks later the Pastor phoned to say that he was not well and needed to focus on treatment for cancer. As such he could not come to the UK. That was a disappointment for us though we recognised that his health had to be the priority in his life, but more than that came the question about George himself. Would he still come to us if his friend was not here? We waited on his reply, wondering what his response might be. George proved to be a man of his word. He had agreed to come and he would keep his promise. George was now the complete team from America, a one man team, but one that came with great talents and abilities. We had no reason to fear, all was going to go well.

I recall meeting George at Edinburgh airport on the Sunday afternoon. George was instantly recognisable and it did not take long for us to discover that despite his international fame he was a very humble man, a real gentleman. George was more than willing to fit into all that was happening. He was the special singing guest on the Sunday evening service despite having little time to acclimatise after his flight in. On the following three days he was to present a gospel concert in the church each evening. Sunday, Monday, Tuesday, and Wednesday were all days in which the church was packed. Yes, George was entertaining, that was his profession, but he was more than that as he faithfully presented his own faith and the people loved him for that. As George left on the Thursday morning he said to me that he would be praying for the people of the town, that he had a heart for them all, and if he could help them again at any time to let him know. Was that just words, or was it something that came sincerely from the heart? The proof of how genuine were his words that came in a letter just a few years later. He wrote saying he would be in Scotland for a series of events, but had one day free, could we use him? Of course we could, but decided we needed a bigger venue. Lochgelly Centre was a bright, modern and attractive community space, including a theatre with over 300 seats. We booked the theatre at a charity rate, and every seat was filled. It was an amazing night. A local politician attended the evening at the theatre and wrote a letter later to say how much he was impressed with everything. He particularly made note of how he was struck on a week leading into Easter that the whole evening reminded him of the relevance of the resurrection and brought a message of hope in a world so much in need of hope.

There is more to come. George Hamilton had a heart attack on September 13, 2014, and died on September 17 at Saint Thomas Midtown Hospital in Nashville. I spoke of how much he appreciated the people of Lochgelly, but the feelings were mutual. Local papers will usually focus on the people and events of the locality, yet this time the headline of the local paper was to highlight the passing of an American singer, raised in North Carolina, who gave his time and his faith to the people of Lochgelly. Thank you George Hamilton IV. In a spirit of humility you came to present the King of Kings.

Since that time I have discovered many singers who made their name in the entertainment world but have since discovered that it is more important to have their name in "the Lambs book of life" as the scriptures would put it. Many of them spoke of an entertainment world where lifestyle was not always the best. One spoke of how the television world would contact him to be the celebrity spokesman for the Atheists in religious debates, but today he is willing to come to churches not merely to sing but also to tell his story of how he met this God that once he denied. One spoke of how he even attempted suicide because the world of fame was not meeting the real need of his life. Today they speak with one voice to say Jesus is Lord! I continue to be amazed at how God gifted these talented people before they ever began their Christian life. Today these people are willing to come to churches irrespective of how small the congregation may be. Some have said to me, "would these people come to us, we are just a small church?" The answer is most definitely yes!

Even more amazing is the people who attend who would not accept an invite to a regular church service, and in the process discover the spiritual answers to their own lives. The singer or the song? It is the song of faith that counts within it all.

Part 3
Barren Rocks or Living Stones?

"FROM BARREN ROCKS ... TO LIVING STONES" is an incident-packed memoir that covers eighteen months in the teenage life of the author in the nineteen sixties

Ministerial opportunities can also come from other sources, and not just the celebrities of life. I remember being approached to conduct a funeral for a lady I had met in a nursing home. I had not met the family before. I was in Scotland and the son lived in England, leaving the daughter to be the contact for all the arrangements. I never met the son till the funeral, so not speaking with him till the tea that followed. As we conversed it turned out that he lived very near to where I had once been as a teenager. I was evacuated out of Aden, South Yemen, in 1967 during a period of extreme terrorism. Part of the coping mechanism of living a nomadic life as a young person meant that you automatically cut off the experiences of the past, one cannot settle in a new environment when continually looking over the shoulder at the places of the past. So as we talked about the area I was conscious that I could not remember the people of that locality. Then a local business was mentioned, and I remembered the family that owned it and mentioned the name. Time had brought changes, it seems, as they said that they are no longer the owners. The conversation continued and then the granddaughter of the deceased came back to us having remembered that was the maiden name of the lady who now owns it with her husband. It was indeed the same family albeit they had now moved into a different generation. I was within months of the age of the lady, so as teenagers we knew each other well. What troubled me was that this was the only one I remembered, especially as my time in the locality was critical for a teenager who had just come out of a dangerous situation. All the others were forgotten. As an adult I have believed that all people we meet should be treasured because in their various ways they have played a role in shaping us into the people that we have become. As I reflected on that I felt that as a young person I had failed to put this ideal into practice. For me there was a sense of disappointment in my failure, yet changing the past is something we cannot do, it has happened and somehow it is something I need to live with.

A few weeks went by and I had taken ill. The Doctors advice was clear, it was time to take it easy, time to prepare and give myself a chance to be renewed. I was not so sure about this. I was used to being active, always another project on the go. I could not grasp the concept of sitting and twiddling my fingers, it just was not me. The church was good, there was no pressure from them to get back into regular pastoral work, but does that mean I do absolutely nothing. I was not so sure. I began remembering the recent experiences and the feelings that I had failed to honour those in my life who had made a difference.

Perhaps this was a chance to address all of that. I sat down in front of the computer and began typing. I wanted to see how much I could remember and where there were gaps I would carry out my research until the whole story was complete. I could not leave these times, places and people in the domain of I do not know. For me it was a therapeutic exercise, and nothing more. By the time it was completed I had put in place my memory of eighteen months of my teenage experiences in Aden and the evacuation back to Suffolk in England. I allowed those that were close to me to read it and each one of them came with the same response which I had not expected. "Why not publish it?" I had written items for magazines and local papers, but never done anything more serious than that when it came to writing. After much pressure and encouragement I followed on the publishing trail using this same writing. The published book was called "From Barren Rocks to Living Stones".

The writing was an inspiration given to me by the ordinary people of my life, but ultimately was to open up other channels of ministry. It was a reminder for me during those difficult moments that God may well use circumstances to open up new possibilities. I was reminded of Joseph, for it seemed that my health at the time was meant for bad, but God turned it into something good. Since the publishing of my book about life in an Arab country I have found many Arabs and people from the Middle East have connected with me on social media. For them it was seen, perhaps, as a means of interacting with someone who knew their history. However, some, though not all, began asking questions as they tried to compare Muslim and Christian lifestyles. This aspect of interacting would not usually be conducted on the public page where their neighbours may see some of their thoughts but by private messaging. I guess that must be the modern equivalent of Nicodemus coming in the night seeking answers to his own spiritual questions, coming at a time when no one could see him. One young lady spoke of her concerns around arranged marriages. Her family had arranged for her to be betrothed to a man she did not know. She felt that she was torn in two, on the one hand she did not wish to disrespect her parents yet this became complicated because she had fallen in love with another young man. It was a real dilemma for her. She wanted to know what the Christian perspectives were on this. Those kinds of questions can be tricky when you know that she needs to live with the consequences of whatever decision is made. Then there was the young man who was asking for a bible. He wanted to know more but could not buy one locally in a Muslim environment.

In another twist some of the friends I met on social Media opened up other avenues of reaching out which I would never have thought possible. One was a journalist who wrote a large spread in the Yemen Post, an English speaking newspaper based in the capital of Yemen, Sana'a. Another journalist wrote an item in Arabic for a newspaper based in Aden in the south of Yemen. Each of these items referred to my writings but also to questions being raised by some my Christian faith. Another person I met through Social Media was the daughter of a member of the Yemen government. It was a surprise to one day receive an invitation to a special Yemen related event based in London. It was as a result of this same lady speaking to her parents and suggesting my involvement. The event was called "Yemen: The hidden jewel", was jointly set up by the Yemen Embassy, London, and the Yemen Media centre. "Yemen: The Hidden Jewel" presented an immersive journey into the rich history, culture, and challenges of Yemen, a nation with untapped potential and hidden treasures. It was a pleasure to be able to accept the invitation and to find ways to relate to these people.

But the greatest pleasure is to be able to build relationships that will be a bridge to bringing people to a relationship in the love of God. This was an experience where I felt I had reached my lowest point, but in the lowest points of life is when we discover what faith is all about, leaning on God, trusting Him we can discover the heights that once seemed impossible.

The psalmist said "Trust (lean on, rely on, and be confident) in the Lord and do good; so shall you dwell in the land and feed surely on His faithfulness, and truly you shall be fed. Delight yourself also in the Lord, and He will give you the desires and secret petitions of your heart." (Psalm 37 verse 3 to 7)

READ NOW!

Also in Paperback

Jon Magee continues to reveal the wealth of story telling that is based upon life experiences within the world

PARADISE ISLAND, HEAVENLY JOURNEY
Jon Magee

CHAPTER 10

Practical suggestions in effective ministry

PART 1
Being full and overflowing?

Pastoral visitation is central in the work of a church that seeks to move forward on the long term and any church or its leadership that fails to address that fails to take the mission of the church seriously. However, there can be dangers if it is not carried out with a measure of wisdom. I will never forget the true story that a lecturer in pastoral studies passed on while I was a student. It is a story that demonstrates how the simple things of life can make a huge difference when it comes to the success or failure of any pastoral ministry.

The lecturer spoke of his friend who had just completed his ministerial training and was beginning his first ministry. To make the story run better I will give the young man the fictitious name of Fred. The name may be fictitious but the rest of the story was certainly true. As one might expect with any young minister starting out in their first charge, Fred was extremely keen and wanted to make a success in all that lay ahead. He set himself an extremely ambitious target that he would visit every member and adherent within a set period of time. Fred was doing very well and was pleased with how everything was going. As he visited the first house he heard the words many other Ministers would have heard before, "Would you like a cup of tea or coffee?" He had heard before how important this was as so many will relax more with the new minister as they have tea or coffee to drink, so he answered yes, with no hesitation. He wanted the people to relax so they could talk and get to know each other better. The process worked a treat and all went well.

After a while he went to the next home that was on the list and the same question emerged once more. He suspected that his people would talk with each other later and maybe compare notes. He feared that he could not appear to be showing any bias, he could not treat anyone different to the others. Besides, the theory had already worked well in the first house so why not in any other house that he visited. Here is an added problem. Because he had set himself a very ambitious target he set out from his house in the morning and planned to spend the whole day visiting. He went from one house to the next house and then to another. Each time there was the same sequence, the same question, and the same answer as Fred agreed to partake of tea or coffee in every visit he made. There is only so much that the human body can take. He was in desperate need to be able to use the toilet but was too shy to ask anyone for permission to use the facilities of the houses he was visiting. Having started out in the morning, moving into the afternoon and then the evening the situation was becoming desperate. He knew he had to get home quickly or he would soon be in big trouble. Despite all of his best effort the reality was that he was not going to get home in time. He stopped his car in a layby, looked around and could see no one, and went behind the nearest tree. Sadly, that was just the beginning of his troubles. Someone had seen him even though he saw nobody, and he was inevitably charged with indecent exposure. That was to be the end of his ministry. A ministry that began with such youthful enthusiasm and desire to do his best, but a ministry that was destined to be very short lived. It was a tragedy for him, to begin with such enthusiasm and yet end with such devastation.

The future of Fred's ministry could have been saved by making a couple of wiser decisions. It is certainly true that people relax more when eating and drinking, but did he need to consume so much? Perhaps there could have been some wisdom in politely saying "no thank you" to at least some of the people he was visiting. Then having found he had consumed too much tea or coffee would it have cost too much to ask to use the toilet facilities in the house. Every human being has these bodily needs, I feel sure that the people that Fred was visiting would have understood his needs.

I have taken these warnings to heart, but have discovered there are further concerns that may prove to be difficult to a young Pastor in exactly the same situation of discerning how to answer to the offer of tea or coffee. My first ministry was in an area that had a large number of whiskey distilleries. There were visits in the community that brought these dangers to light. The people were always keen to show good hospitality. So even if they did not attend the church they wanted to show that they would give the Minister the best. If they were given too much advance warning it could easily become like a state visit with a full spread on the table, which is far too much. The first question I would be asked would be "Would you like a cup of tea?" I had already had my fill of hospitality for the day so I would politely decline the offer. The next question would be "Would you like a cup of coffee then?" I would reply "No thank you". It is at this point that having declined both tea and coffee then they understood what I was really wanting. So they offered something harder. "Would you prefer a dram of whiskey then?" So I decided that it may be better to take the risk of too much tea or coffee rather than too much whiskey. Taking that line of course means emphasising even more that we must not be too shy when it comes to asking people if we can use their facilities before moving on to the next visit. I have not had my request refused at any time. It seems to be such a small thing, but as we have learnt can make all the difference between facing a full ministry or no ministry at all. It is no small sacrifice, it seems, when placed in that perspective. Wisdom is essential in ministry. James says "If any of you lacks wisdom, you should ask God, who gives generously to all without finding fault, and it will be given to you." This is one of the Bible verses about wisdom and guidance that remind us of the importance of asking God to show us His views, His perspective and His standards.

Part 2
Disruptions in the services

I recall as a student preaching in a church in a Glasgow housing scheme. I was in the midst of my sermon, right at the heart of the whole theme of the service, when all the Deacons suddenly made a quick exit from the building. It was a natural thought for me, what have I said that caused such a drastic reaction. I really did not think there was anything that was in any way heretical in what I was saying. I was pretty sure that my theology was what it should be. There was nothing offensive in what was said. So what was the cause of the disruption?

Drumchapel in the 1970's was tougher than almost anywhere

else in Scotland. It makes you wonder why the builders thought a flat roofed building was the correct design. Apart from the issues of heavy rain in the west of Scotland here was a building that was in the midst of a tough housing scheme where young teenagers were always on the lookout for new forms of entertainment and challenges. So a flat roofed building was a place that seemed to be very inviting for them to climb up and find a new play centre. The fact that a worship service was taking place in the building was a minor detail, even at such a time of this they would take this challenge as being something to respond to. The Deacons had gone, not to escape the service but out of concern for the safety of the young people that were playing on the roof.

There are times when disruption can come from within the congregation. On another Sunday I was preaching at the very same building. This time none of the Deacons left the building. This time there was a completely different concern. A young lady became unwell, we will give her the name of Lucy, though that was not her real name. Lucy was epileptic and during the service she took an epileptic fit. Epilepsy is a common condition that affects the brain and causes frequent seizures. Seizures are bursts of electrical activity in the brain that temporarily affect how it works. They can cause a wide range of symptoms. Epilepsy can start at any age, but usually starts either in childhood or in people over 60. It's often lifelong, but can sometimes get slowly better over time. Seizures can affect people in different ways, depending on which part of the brain is involved.

I had no prior knowledge of her health issues, I just heard a noise from one part of the congregation and saw her friends trying to assist her.

In both these situations what is the role of the preacher? The show business world would say "the show must go on". I am not sure that is quite how I or any preacher would phrase it, but the principle is still the same. Lucy did not need the attention of the whole congregation. That would be detrimental to the well being of Lucy. Too many people gathering around her would deprive the patient of oxygen and increase her embarrassment when she would later come out of the fit. The immediate friends would have the role of supporting Lucy and ensuring she is kept safe and not hurt by nearby furniture. The role of the preacher is to keep everyone calm and focused on what they are in the church for. From memory I think that I did take a moment to pray for Lucy, and then to continue to lead the worship and the service for those not actively caring for Lucy. In any gathering of people there will always be a risk of someone being unwell and the same principles need to be addressed.

As for the time where the young people were playing on the church roof, the same principle needs to apply. The Deacons had the issues under control, the Preacher has the role of keeping the congregation calm. They need to be distracted from the chaos on the roof and focused on the Christ who is at the heart of the worship. Jesus said *""God is a Spirit: and they that worship Him must worship Him in spirit and in truth" (John 4 verse 24)*. Here is where we need to focus irrespective of whatever distractions may surround us.

Part 3
Knowing the community

Before taking up my first charge, which was on Islay, in the Hebrides, I recall having a conversation with one of the older members of the church. The island had two Baptist churches, which at that time were completely autonomous but sharing the same Minister. Phame spoke from the heart as she voiced some of her concerns. In the midst of this vital conversation Phame said, "You know, some people think we do not have a Minister, there is just the Bowmore Minister who drives across to help us and then leaves. No one sees him". I understood where she was coming from and knew there needed to be some way of addressing that. I was determined that this was something I must never forget. The island was about twenty by thirty miles in size, and the two churches were ten miles apart, so there was a real challenge for me. So how was the challenge met? I decided that I would not drive door to door on any visitation. Once I reached the beginnings of a community I would park the car and then walk to any house I was visiting. As I did so then I found there were people who were willing to talk. Island life is like that. You may talk about a whole multitude of things before reaching what was really on the heart, but if one is prepared to talk on these terms then many doors would be opened. If I can draw a comparison between the law and the grace, many senior members of British life will bemoan the fact that the bobby on the beat is no longer seen. They are driving around, but are not seen. In the same way the Minister needed to be seen. During my five and a half years ministry on the island I endeavoured to exercise an island wide ministry visiting each of the communities. By using the principle of walking in this way meant I was seen. The slower the mode of transport the less one might do, but it was important that the little that was done was seen to be done. For every Minister we each need to find a way to overcome the challenges that surround us. The challenges may differ, but here is one way in which I tried to meet the island challenge.

Exercising such a ministry on an island does mean a measure of sacrifice, one of which is privacy. One day we decided to take a break and visit Ardtalla. There was no village or community there, so we saw it as a chance of just being a family. Ardtalla Beach is one of Islay's Hidden Gems and the trip to Ardtalla is about as good as it gets on Islay. It's a ten mile trip up the stunning south-eastern coast of Islay, well away from everywhere. We had a great time enjoying the beach. Ardtalla Beach is just one of those stunning places you don't want to leave, especially on a warm and sunny day which was the case this day. Later on in the day we called into a shop twenty miles away in Bowmore and were greeted with the words "I hear you were in Ardtalla today". We learned a lot that day. There was no hiding place.

In each of my subsequent ministries I made a point of walking around the area. I gave priority on arriving to walking around and discovering as much as I could and meeting the people. If one wants to give the best to an area one needs to get to know the area and its people. I cannot emphasise more how important it is to start a ministry like that. In terms of knowing the people, that can include meeting them in the context of community groups as well as walking through the community. If the community is to know that we care about them and desire to support them then they need to be able to see our availability for them.

God always uses those who are available. In the late 50's a country preacher named David Wilkerson began travelling from Pennsylvania to New York City to reach gang members who were steeped in murder & violence. Eventually reaching one of the most notorious gang members at the time, a teenager named Nicky Cruz.

How did David Wilkerson become the one to reach these gang members? I'm sure there were others who were far more capable to reach them.

I believe one of the primary qualifications was availability.

Bob Goff puts it this way: "God often uses the least qualified, most available people to get things done." Like Peter, the other disciples and many others whom God has used, availability was an initiator for God to great things through their life. I wonder what could God do in your life because of a decision to show up. What could God do in the life of others because you decided to be available. Availability makes room for the miraculous. In the following passage notice how the Bible makes mention of two boats being docked.

One day as Jesus was standing by the Lake of Gennesaret, the people were crowding around him and listening to the word of God. He saw at the water's edge **two boats**, *left there by the fishermen, who were washing their nets. He got into one of the boats, the* **one belonging to Simon (Peter)**, *and asked him to put out a little from shore. Then he sat down and taught the people from the boat..."* Luke 5:1-3 (NIV)

Consider this: Jesus ASKED Peter to put his boat further out into the water: Could Peter have said no? Could he have resisted? If Peter had said no or resisted, could Jesus have used the other boat? Of course He could have. Figuratively speaking, is Jesus asking to use your boat? Is there something in your life that God is asking you to use on His behalf? It could be a resource, talent, ability, or anything else He has entrusted to you that He wants to use?

Read what happened next...

"...When he had finished speaking, he said to Simon (Peter), "Put out into deep water, and let down the nets for a catch." Simon answered, "Master, we've worked hard all night and haven't caught anything. But because you say so, I will let down the nets." When they had done so, they caught such a large number of fish that their nets began to break. Luke 5:4-6 (NIV)

For Jesus to use the boat meant that Peter would have

to stop what he was doing (washing the nets). Peter would need to prep the boat to sail back out into the waters… he'd have to drop anchor again. In other words, it was seemingly inconvenient and not worth it. But take note of his response to Jesus' request. "Master, we've worked hard all night and haven't caught anything. But **because you say so,** I will let down the nets."

Part 4
Knowing the people.

Just as it is important to know the community it is equally important to know the people we serve and to give them the opportunity to know the Minister. The Minister and congregation will never know each other by merely talking on the doorstep of the church. To fail to grasp that fact is looking at a limited ministry. Pastoral visits will not be the best if it's just about visiting in a time of need. A church needs to be receptive to regular visits long before that, taking time to know the heart of each other, if the later needs are ever to be fully met. It is during these times that they can discover items that they may have in common. For example, there have been occassions when I have visited homes where the wife attended faithfully but the husband did not. When visiting for the first time the husband was not in anyway disrespectful but there was an assumption, it seemed, that the minister was there visiting the faithful, not himself. However, when the conversation continued it was found that both he and I had a background in the Royal Air Force. The eyes lit up at this point, we had something in common. From that point on he looked forward to the visits, even requesting not to forget to pray for him. Later, he began attending on a Sunday, even if his wife was not well enough to come he still came on his own. He developed an enthusiasm, asking specific questions related to matters of faith, and then attending the bible studies. He desperately was looking for answers, seeking to know how he could advance on his spiritual journey of life. There are, of course, many other examples that could be drawn on these things. It is also an opportunity for both the Pastor and the church member to understand the weaknesses of each other, or the questions that could not be answered in the public Sunday Service. The private pastoral visit is sometimes the more appropriate place, and those questions will come easier when each takes time to get to know each other. The hopes of our future partnership of the gospel begins at this point as we give time to each other.

The pastor needs the ability to interact with people in a friendly way and with courtesy, compassion, and empathy. He needs to be "others oriented" as opposed to being self-absorbed or task driven. He needs to notice people (without looking past them) and look them in the eye and smile. He needs to be able to call the people of his congregation by name like Jesus said a good shepherd does (John chapter 10 verse 3). The pastor must interact with people and ask sincere questions demonstrating concern, communicating both verbally and non-verbally in ways that demonstrate courtesy and love for each other. The pastor needs to be able to listen effectively, handle difficult conversations, discipline his anger, and help resolve conflict. These are all important aspects to remember as we speak of the relationship between one seeking to give pastoral help an the congregation.

Part 5
Being a prayerful encouragement but never a discouraging critic.

Billy Graham, an American evangelist, has certainly been one person that has had a tremendous influence on evangelical Christianity in the United Kingdom in the late 20th century. Indeed many who rose to leading positions in the church in the UK have spoken of how their spiritual life was enhanced through the Billy Graham organisation. Likewise Billy Graham also appeared to enjoy his visits to the UK. David Vardy, who was executive chairman of the Billy Graham Evangelistic Association (BGEA) says: "He calls the UK his 'second home.'"

I had a number of opportunities to be involved with Billy Graham missions during my ministry and I remember specifically what was destined to be his last visit to the UK. Billy Graham returned to Scotland in 1991 with meetings in Edinburgh, Aberdeen, and Glasgow. The numbers this time were lower than his visit in 1955 and the delivery was more measured. The message, however, was just the same, "Give your life to Jesus Christ!" Just as in 1955 people were not only brought to faith but some were also called into Christian service so the impact lay not only in the generation that came forward on the day but for generations that lay ahead. My involvement on this occasion in 1991 was with the team of counsellors at two of these venues. In Edinburgh we gathered at the home of Scottish Rugby, Murrayfield, and in Glasgow it was at the home of Celtic football in Glasgow. I remember having a conversation with a friend at the time when it was noted that the preaching seemed different to previous visits. The thinking and delivery appeared slower, and with hindsight it would seem that his health had detrimentally affected him by this time. Yet as the appeal was given the crowds still responded. Wave after wave of people came forward inspired to make a life changing decision for Christ, the most important decision they would make in their lifetime. Clearly the Holy Spirit was still powerfully at work whatever may be happening in this human body and despite any criticism we may make. I have always felt that this was an important lesson that we all need to learn. As a preacher we may feel we have some justification in criticising a man who is faithfully giving their heart for the Lord's work, but that's not what God has called us to do. Whoever we may work with our role should be to act as encouragement. If we see ourselves as a self appointed critic, and particularly when done in a manner that can only discourage, then we have failed to grasp what the Lord may be doing. This is particularly the case in the local church scene where folks may be needing some guidance that comes with compassion. It's an opportunity for them to grow. However, if they receive a barrage by one who has no real understanding of compassion it will often result in people falling back rather than moving forward in their Christian service. It is even worse when it is done publicly, and the world looks on and asks where is the Christians love for others. If we are here merely to be the criticisers then we have failed to understand the calling of the God who has set us apart to declare the love of God.

The bible has some insights on the importance of being an encourager rather than finding reasons to be critical. Barnabas was an encourager. In the Scriptures, he is singled out as a believer who encouraged others by his generosity (Acts chapter 4 verse 36 to 37). He encouraged Paul, as is seen in Acts chapter 9 verse 27 which reads "But Barnabas took [Saul] and brought him to the apostles." He also played a critical role in encouraging

John Mark, a young man who was deemed an unreliable failure by Paul because he had abandoned the first missionary journey. Barnabas wanted to take John Mark on the second missionary trip, but Paul refused, causing a severe break in their partnership. Barnabas took a big risk and gave John Mark a second chance, restoring him to effective ministry.

Before we move on from talking about Billy Graham I would like to speak of another experience. In a previous mission when I lived near Glasgow there was to be a satelite link from England. Though we were linked by satelite each area that was linked had to arrange its own administration. There was a need for someone to be involved with public relations. I volunteered to be considered and we were given training at a local Christian radio station. The station, Gospel Radio Fellowship, or GRF, made high-quality thought-provoking and entertaining radio programmes and podcasts that aim to engage the listener by exploring spirituality from the perspective of the Christian faith. Made by a small team of volunteers, all of their programmes aimed to give audiences an experience to take them on a journey and discover new dimensions of faith. The programmes were broadcast on radio stations in Britain and throughout the world. Many of them were also suitable as audio resources for schools and churches. What was crucial for us was that they had a team of talented volunteers who were able to provide bespoke training on all aspects of radio production.

So they put us through all the training and then made the decision who would be suitable to be interviewed by the media at any given time. In short, it was not to be me. This was not to be my time for radio work. However, this time was invaluable in preparing me for the time when that would be a possibility later in my ministry. We all need to learn that the time is not always right for what we desire to do in the Lords work, but we must take the opportunities of learning on the way.

Part 6
Listen to the doctor orders.

I said that the last time Billy Graham came to the UK was in 1991. What I never said was that this mission was very nearly the last time I would be involved in any kind of ministry. The three venues were collectively known as Mission Scotland and there was an air of excitement throughout Scotland as the time approached. I had personally enjoyed the time in Edinburgh as we shared the good news. Then came the time in Glasgow as we gathered in Celtic Park.

For many football fans it will seem like paradise to walk on the turf at Celtic Park. I say that with a touch of irony. The Park is also known as *Parkhead* or *Paradise*. As one responsible for a team of counsellors I walked on the turf of Paradise every day I was there. Just as it was in Edinburgh so it was here, the enquirers just kept coming forward and we took up our positions as we talked with them and answered their questions. There was a more important paradise they needed, not one based on football, but one based on the eternal promises of our Lord. We stayed with them till all had been counselled irrespective of how long that would take.

I recall that on one of those days at Celtic Park the heavens opened and the rain descended in a way that could only happen in the west of Scotland. Despite that we kept our stand as we would on any other day. However, this was just the beginning of a spiritual battle regarding my personal involvement in "Mission Scotland".

Over the next few days I began to feel quite ill. I was not

sure what was happening with my body. I wondered if I had developed a cold, a reasonable conclusion I thought having spent so long in the rain, yet there seemed to be something more. It all started off with what seemed like a cough, coughing up some mucus or phlegm. I developed a shortness of breath which in itself was worrying, but there was more to come, it seemed. My body was aching and I was feeling very tired. I was making wheezing noises when I breathed. Even more worrying was an extremely strong chest pain. The chest pain was getting worse, particularly as I coughed. It became clear that I was needing help, and I needed it soon. So it happened that as the Sunday morning arrived so I was to arrive at the Edinburgh Royal Infirmary instead of my usual preaching in the local church. I was in no fit medical state to be preaching anywhere, that was clear.

The hospital began to carry out various tests. They began by giving me blood tests including a complete blood count. They also began checking how much oxygen was in my blood. Finally they ordered a chest x-ray. It appears they were looking for inflammation in my lungs.

What was the conclusion to it all? The doctor appeared by my bedside looking very serious, which was not too reassuring for me at the time. He explained all the tests that had been done and showed me the chest x-ray, pointing out what could be seen in my chest. I could not understand everything that was said, but when I heard the word pneumonia I realised that this was something serious, it could not be treated lightly. It was more than a cold. I assumed, wrongly, that this was something that was for people older and not so fit, so it was a shock to me. The doctor was of the same mind that this was serious. He said that the medical world can give the treatment but the patient must be prepared to take life easy if it is all to work. When it came to the time of my discharge I was given a "sick line" and told that this was not going to be enough time, this will need to be extended when that time expires. I remember explaining all this to the church secretary and seeing his face falling in the midst of all that. He could not see how he and the church could cope. He was troubled, not knowing what to do. Seeing this reaction, despite all that I had experienced at the hospital, I began to feel guilty, guilty that I had let them all down. They were depending on me, it seems, and so I never took the extended time the doctors recommended. On reflection, I was wrong. The doctor was clear that there were real dangers if his guidance was not followed. I was fortunate, despite the warnings God gave protection to me during this time. However, if I had followed the doctor's guidance then it is the same God who needed to be trusted to protect the church. Since then I have been clear in my mind that when a church leadership disagrees with a doctor on medical matters then the doctor's view must always be given priority. If a church leadership assumes they have the authority to monitor a medical situation when the doctor says otherwise then they have failed to understand their role. As the Minister it is equally important for us to have the same understanding. For me this could have been the end of my ministry, and as ministry is God's call then it will be wrong to bring it to an end through an act of foolishness."God made your body, Jesus died for your body, and He expects you to take care of your body."

There are some interesting quotes we all need to heed:

"Take care of your body. It's your only place to live."

"Everything God makes has a purpose."

Scripture tells us to take care of our bodies. Taking care of the body that the Lord has given you is another form of honoring the Lord. It is revealing a heart that is grateful for what God has given them. You want to be prepared physically to do whatever God calls you to do.

Part 7
Try Praying!

A number of women in my first ministry on the island of Islay gathered together for prayer. Through out history women gathered in prayer have shown themselves to be a powerful force in Gods kingdom. I am sure that these ladies on the island were a modern demonstration of this as they prayed for every need in Gods work. Let me speak of one area where they prayed about what seemed to be the basic needs, and the way in which God would answer.

The ladies loved the opportunity for worship and felt that a piano in the Bowmore church would help to enhance the worship. There was an old organ but no piano. It was a small church and so the material resources were limited, but they knew they had a mighty God, and so they met to pray. When God is in the equation we are never limited on the grand scale of things. Time went by, but undaunted the ladies kept their focus on pleading with God in their regular prayer sessions. They were confident that in Gods time the answer would be given. Believing prayer is essential in Christian work. Meanwhile, just two doors away from the church God was at work. A lady who at the time had no connection with the church had a question she needed answered. She was unaware of the prayer sesions and what was being prayed for. She had a piano, just what the ladies had been praying for, but it was badly in need of tuning. It was her daughters but her daughter no longer had an interest in playing. "Would the church be interested in the piano?" she asked.

The piano may not be tuned, but it was a piano and the God that the ladies had pleaded to could deal with that too. So the piano was wheeled along the street from the house to the church. There it lay, unplayed, while the ladies now prayed for a tuner. What miracles would the Lord now provide? During the coming summer we were looking forward to a mission team coming from a church in Ayr. The leader of the team, John Rob, phoned me one day to talk about his hopes and aspirations. In the midst of our conversation John spoke of a member of the team who was a wonderful pianist. He said "I would love to be able to use her talents when we come, do you have a piano in the church?" Of course we have a piano, but it is in need of being tuned. I then explained to John how the ladies had prayed for a piano and what happened as a result of those prayers. John was amazed at all that I shared with him and immediately responded by saying "Let us continue in partnership, we will also pray for a piano tuner and together we will see great things happening". Prayer must always be the answer.

A week later John phoned me once again. He said "Jon, I think we have part of the answer. I have someone who is a very good tuner. He would be pleased to assist, but he has a very heavy work load. We need to find a way to get him over to the island in a way in which he can still manage for him to get back to his work the same day. Please continue to pray, God has an answer." And so the prayers continued. A miracle was in the process of being revealed. It was just a couple of weeks later when the answer to prayer was taken another step forward. A member of the church in Ayr was a retired airline pilot who had regularly flown airlines across the Atlantic. Despite being retired he continued to love flying. In order that he keep his flying licence it was important for him to keep up his flying hours, and every opportunity to fly he would grab it. "God is at work, keep praying" said Rob.

The day was fixed for the piano tuner to be flown over, and then came the disappointment. The weather that morning was not suitable for flying. It was on the third attempt to fly that the weather was to prove to be satisfactory. The piano tuner was flown over, he completed the task and was home in time to finish his professional work the same day. God can indeed do miraculous work, why should we be surprised that God who created the universe cannot do something of this nature? It was that week that a very accomplished pianist came to the island to attend a wedding that I was officiating at. Hearing about the piano he struggled to understand what was happening. How can a small church manage to fly a piano tuner across from the mainland for just one job and then return him the same day to complete his working day? He could not comprehend how this was possible. However, when we know the God we are speaking of then we know that even greater miracles can be possible.

There are many Biblical references that encourage us to pray when we are faced with uncertainty or discomfort. Sometimes all we can do is trust in God and have faith in Him when things are out of our control. Prayer is an act of that trust and faith that God will answer our calls and provide what is best for us. It is also an act of gratitude, as we pray in appreciation for what God has given us. Paul writes to the Philippians " Do not be anxious about anything, but in every situation, by prayer and petition, with thanksgiving, present your requests to God." (Philippians chapter 4 verse 6)

Part 8
Can the World see the work of God?

That is an interesting question. I will come back to it shortly but in the meanwhile let me take you back to a typical summer on Islay in the 1980's. For many Ileachs, or natives of Islay, a typical day would be spent cutting the peat on the peat bank. A bank could be rented for about £7 or £8 a year and so if you were unemployed and had the spare time it is possible to ensure one has a full winters heating for a relatively small amount of money. I had a peat bank myself, I never managed to cut sufficient for a full winter but the other advantage I found was that it was a place I could go to and be undisturbed as I sought to think and pray and discern the sermon for the coming Sunday. Meanwhile, in the community if it was a good sunny day the ladies might be seen putting out the washing to dry on the clothes line. Either activity it was important to have a dry sunny day. Yet the weather was something that we have little control over. We plan our activity, we hope, but the weather is in the hand of God.

Now what is the church activity during this time in the 1980's? The church set up "Tea on the Green" in Port Ellen, on the south of the island. Port Ellen was the main port for the island and saw many visitors passing through. The Tea on the Green was not every week, but as often as circumstances allowed. The tables and chairs were set up outside the Macaulay and Torrie shop, as it was at the time, very close to the church in Port Ellen. It was at one end of Frederick Crescent overlooking the bay and the pier, and the activity taking place could be seen all the way around the bay. Mary Macaulay who part owned the shop was the main organiser of what was happening. The event was well supported by the local people, indeed they looked forward to it making it a priority for them when the tables appeared on a Wednesday afternoon. For myself it was a good pastoral opportunity with the community as they came to us, sat with us, and we talked and listened to each other as we had a cup of tea or coffee.

What about the weather? We said earlier that mankind has no control over it yet here is an activity which good weather is essential if it is to be a success. Yet it was most certainly a success. It often happened that the day in which the teas were planned the rain would fall. It could be raining all morning yet in faith everyone focused on the plan they had for the afternoon. As the tables were set up, amazingly the sun came out and shone brightly. The sunny weather would continue through the rest of the afternoon, but once the tables were removed the sunny weather could not be relied on to remain.

The world looked on in wonder. The first that I realised how the community were thinking was when a man stopped his bicycle when he saw me, looked me in the face, and said "Mr Magee, could you tell me when you will have the next Tea on the Green? I am desperate for good weather so I can work on my peat bank". Soon after that I discovered that ladies were raising similar questions, but for them the need was for a good afternoon to dry the washing. How do we respond to this? We can debate as to whether the Lord would change the weather for the sake of a gathering for tea on the green. However, there was no doubt that people were recognising the power of God in a way they had not done before. Once again, as the community makes their observations should we not also take the opportunity to speak of our mighty God. There is a childrens chorus that says "My God is so big, so strong, so mighty there's nothing that He cannot do!" If the world can recognise the power of God then even more so should one who has been given salvation by the power and the grace of our God.

The psalmist said "Come and see what God has done, his awesome deeds for mankind!" Praise God that the world can see, and in this sight they can believe.

Part 9
Never write a person off as being impossible

At one time whilst in Edinburgh I would take turns with other Ministers in leading a weekly service in a Nursing Home on a Sunday afternoon. It was the Tor Nursing Home. The TOR Christian Nursing Home was home to fifty people in the leafy area of Murrayfield in Edinburgh, very near the Murrayfield Rugby stadium. One of the elderly ladies, Mrs. Daunt, would usually sit at the back, but being at the back did not stop her from being heard. It did not matter who the minister was she would make sure all could hear as she heckled through out the service. We understood that this related to her health, sadly she was suffering from dementia. So we carried on despite the heckling, it was not her fault and we needed to remember that we were there to present the love of God.

One Sunday I noticed a dramatic change. This week there was no heckling which we had come to expect. This time instead of heckling Mrs Daunt cried and cried throughout the service. At the close of the service I went and sat down beside her and talked with her and listened to what she had to say. She explained the reason for her crying. As she listened to the hymn singing she was reminded how she sat on her mothers knee as her mother taught her to sing hymns and choruses.

The memories had come flooding back as she was filled with emotions. A stranger listening to the heckling could be forgiven for thinking that there was no spirituality in the life of Mrs. Daunt, but now I was seeing and listening to a completely different lady. It was as if she had been struggling to work through a mental filing system for all these years, but now all was revealed. It was soon after this incident that Mrs. Daunt was to pass away. I am confident that on the day she passed was the day she joined a heavenly choir. The heckling was from the past, the present was about praising her Lord and her God. Not one person, not even Mrs Daunt, should be dismissed as worthless, not worth trying to help. She had the Lord hidden within her frail human body and now she possesses a glorious body the Lord has promised her.

As Isaiah wrote, "But they who wait for the Lord shall renew their strength; they shall mount up with wings like eagles; they shall run and not be weary; they shall walk and not faint" (Isaiah chapter 40 verse 31).

Part 10
Back to the future

The year was 1986, but amazingly we were about to be transported back in time to the nineteenth century! None of us expected that this was going to be our experience as we woke that morning. How on earth could that be possible? Yet amazingly it really was about to happen.

The Bowmore church was seriously in need of renovation. There was so much work to do but fortunately the manpower was available from within the church membership. So the work began. For me there was a number of eye openers. The floor boards were lifted and as I looked underneath all that I could see was earth. Where were the foundations? How does this fit with my theology? For years I had preached sermons on the importance of having a strong and sure foundation. The most obvious scriptural passage was the parable of the wise man and the foolish man. The wise man worked hard digging the foundations in the rock and when the storms came the house and the rock stood firm. The foolish man saw no need to work so hard, so he built his house on the sand. The house looked wonderful, but when the storms blew the house on the sand fell flat. Now how does that fit with what I was now seeing? I am so glad that one of the men more familiar with building work took me on one side and pointed to the walls. The walls were huge. They must have been a good couple of feet wide, and faithfully those walls kept everything together. There was the foundation that had seen the building through the centuries.

There was an even deeper revelation that was coming, however. John McNeill was working beneath the pulpit when he came across an amazing discovery. John pulled out a green bottle and with excitement shared with us his outstanding discovery. It was a time capsule that had been placed under the pulpit in 1869 when work was previously carried out on the church. In that moment we, in a sense, went back in time as we examined the time capsule hidden beneath a pulpit where week by week the good news of the Saviour had been preached so faithfully.

Back in 1869 the faithful saints of that time had also been carrying out essential work on the building. At the same time they wanted to find a way to look forward and share what was on their hearts to the generations that would follow them.

Psalm 78 champions the truth that the older members of God's community are called to pass their faith to the next generation. Asaph's Psalm carries this idea of passing the baton of faith to children who then teach their children as well so that they should hope in God and remember His works. *We will not conceal them from their children, but tell to the generation to come the praises of the Lord, and His strength and His wondrous works that He has done. For He established a testimony in Jacob and appointed a law in Israel, which He commanded our fathers that they should teach them to their children, that the generation to come might know, even the children yet to be born, that they may arise and tell them to their children, that they should put their confidence in God and not forget the works of God, but keep His commandments. (Psalm 78:4-7).*

Chapter 11

Going the extra mile

Part 1
Ben Vicar

Are we willing to go outside of our comfort zone? I am of the opinion that sometimes we need to do so. That may not be easy to do but if we wish to reach out we need to be prepared to be in the comfort zone of others, not ourselves. We need to be willing to put them at ease if they are going to listen to the message that is dear to our heart. Tom, a ministerial colleague, was coming to Islay to assist us with some special youth meetings. The youth events were not meant to be restricted to church youth but community youth. So as part of our preparations we took time to research where the youth were and sent out special personal invitations to each of the young people. We wanted them to feel welcome to all that we were doing. At the same time it is important to always remember that each of the young people do not come alone, they are part of a wider family.

I recall visiting one family that lived outside of the community to offer an invitation to the young people. It was a long drive to the house itself, with rabbits running freely around. I reached the house and knocked on the door, wondering to myself what kind of reaction I would get as I trespassed on their home land, but my hope was that it would be appreciated that we cared for the young people and wanted the best for each of them. The door was opened, I introduced myself, and was invited in. The welcome was more than I could have imagined. I spoke with the lady of the house, Fiona, and one of the teenagers as we sat and had coffee together. After a while another teenager came into the room and said that dad, George, was coming down to meet me. I think we were all surprised about that as George preferred to have his own space, and not be disturbed. I guess that it helped that the young people were aware that I had visited the school and had seen me and heard me speaking there at the school.

George was an interesting character. He was a runner and was known to take part in the Bens of Jura fell race. It is one of the toughest challenges in British hill racing at this distance, it's a long, tough and very rough race. To compete in such a race is an indicator of the runner being extremely fit. Only the very fit were acceptable to compete. He spoke of some of his interests including running. We also spoke about spiritual concerns. This was to be the first of many conversations that we were to share, and so a visit to meet the needs of teenagers was to encompass the needs of the next generation. It was during one of these conversations that I said, "George, some time when you are going on your training route could I go with you?" I must have had a fit of madness since I had no experience in running, so I quickly added that as we took the route I would prefer to walk, not run. George agreed, with the qualification that it would only happen when he felt it was the right time. I then put it all to the back of my mind.

It was early January first thing in the morning as I heard the telephone ring. I had looked out of the window to see the wintry snow falling. I picked up the phone to hear a voice saying, "Jon, I think this is the right day for us to go on the training route." Yes, it was George, and my mad suggestion was coming home to roost. We were going to make our way up Ben Vicar. Beinn Bheigeir (occasionally anglicised as "Ben Vicar"), it is the highest of the seven 'Marilyn' hills on Islay, and the highest point on the island. It stands at 491 metres, or 1,611 feet, and being an island the climb begins at sea level. I am so pleased that by the time we started the ascent the snow had ceased to fall and due to the salt air frost does not last long.

As we reached the summit we looked around and admired the tremendous view that lay before us. On a clear day views from this spot would include the island of Jura with the Paps of Jura, Kintyre, the Isle of Arran and most of the island of Islay. This was indeed a clear day and as George pointed out the various places before us I could see why this was such an important place for him. We had walked up as I had suggested in the beginning, but as we went down again we broke into a trot and soon reached the bottom. We sat in the vehicle at the botto and talked. It was probably the best conversation I had ever had with George, but as is so often the case for him to open up, it required a willingness to understand what was important to him even if that meant stepping outside of my own "comfort zone". From my perspective this is crucial, if we want people to listen to our message we need to be prepared to take the risks in life.

Thinking through this particular experience I also take note that I am speaking of people who not only had an interest in running but also in what is happening in creation. The writer to the Romans makes it clear that we cannot look to the creation without acknowledging that there is a creator. Paul writes "since what may be known about God is plain to them, because God has made it plain to them. For since the creation of the world God's invisible qualities—his eternal power and divine nature—have been clearly seen, being understood from what has been made, so that people are without excuse." (Romans chapter 1 verses 19 and 20). As such by looking into the realm of creation comes the opportunity of sharing the good news. The God who loves the creation he has given has also demonstrated his love for us as he gave his son for us.

Part 2
Kildalton

"George, with the wild life on his estate.
Painting by Suyeon Kim"

There were going to be many more conversations with George and Fiona. George and Fiona were the owners of the Kildalton estate. I will later speak of the personal connections

I had with Kildalton historically, but for now lets focus on the events of the time. George and Fiona had very strong views on conservation and environmental issues. I remember the time when George asked me if the church in Port Ellen would like a gift of a Christmas tree as Christmas approached. I thanked him for his kindness and said that such a gift would be very much appreciated. I then put the idea to the back of my mind and carried on with the daily tasks of ministry. As Advent arrived I had a most wondrous surprise to see a huge Christmas tree placed inside the church grounds. This must be the tree promised by George, I thought, as the tree was carried inside the building. I said the tree was huge, the church had a ceiling that was high enough to equate to a two story building and the tree filled the full height of the church. Then began the task of decorating the tree. How we managed to decorate the top of the tree I have no idea, but the work was completed. The top was important thats where the star was placed, symbolically a reminder of the star of 2,000 years ago pointing the wise men in the direction of Jesus, the son of God who came in the flesh at Bethlehem. Christmas means nothing if we cannot use the time to point to the Christ child who came to give us new life.

Later, I was to get a large shock as George came to me with a confession. George looked me in the eye and said "Jon, I am sorry, I promised you a tree but later I regretted making such a promise. With my environmental beliefs I could not bring myself to cut the tree down." I began the process in my mind trying to work through the implications of this confession. If George had not donated the tree then who did the tree belong to? Have we illegally taken possession of a tree that belonged to someone else? Would we now have to remove the decorations and pass the tree to someone else? So many questions with no answers. I was feeling a little guilty wondering what may lie ahead. It was then that George explained what he meant. He had indeed had a rethink, but had come up with an alternative plan that suited his views on the environment. At some point in the past a tree had been struck by lightning. It subsequently lay on its side though still with its roots in the ground. From this fallen tree a branch had grown, and as would happen in nature the branch sought to grow towards the light. It did not stop growing till it had succeeded in its goal. The huge "tree" we had decorated in the church was really just a branch born out of what seemed like a disaster for the tree. For me there seemed to be a lot of symbolism that was springing forth from this story. It was Christmas, when we celebrate the birth of one whose mission was to die on the cross of calvary in order that we might know life by trusting Jesus as our Saviour and Lord. The branch grew out of disaster, our lives grow out of the Jesus struck down for us at Calvary.

As I write I am concious that Wilding and Rewilding is the modern trend, but long before it became fashionable the Kildalton estate had already established this as the policy of the estate. Rewilding is a progressive approach to conservation. It's about letting nature take care of itself, enabling natural processes to shape land and sea, repair damaged ecosystems and restore degraded landscapes. Through rewilding, wildlife's natural rhythms create wilder, more biodiverse habitats. When nature is healthy, we are healthier too. We rely on the natural world for water, food and air. There is a growing realisation that connecting with wild nature makes us feel good and keeps us mentally and physically well. Rewilding is about trusting the forces of nature to restore land and sea. This is something of the thinking of George and Fiona regarding their estate.

The seals also come into their concerns. Fiona specifically set up a seal sanctuary on the estate as she rescued seals that were sick, caring for them, nursing them, until they were strong enough and fit to be released into the sea once more. It is all about preparing the seals to fend for themselves as they return to the wild life of nature. Fiona also used her musical skills in bringing comfort to the people of the sea. As has been noted in the wider media Fiona has often stood on the coastline playing her violin, and the seals would come and gather round to listen as she played. Now, why am I speaking about this in the context of a book called "Confessions of a Baptist Minister"? Well, I confess that as Christians we all need to address the responsibilities that God has placed upon us. In Genesis God gives to man the honour of naming the creatures that have been created. Giving names in the ancient east was important. It was effectively an opportunity to claim dominion over the ones being named. In the modern world we think of dominion as being about us, about us claiming our rights over creation and the animals within the world. However, dominion means more than that, it means we have a responsibility to care for those we have dominion over. If we do not care about the creation that surrounds us then we have failed in what God intends for us. In addition Genesis chapter verse 26 states that God gave humans dominion over the earth and all living things, including animals, birds, and fish. The word "dominion" means "rule or power over", but it's more about stewardship and caretaking than ownership and control. God's command to subdue the earth is seen as a blessing, and it includes responsibilities such as: caring for animals and using them in a just way, managing animals humanely, and not mistreating or misusing animals.

In that context, can we ever forget that God gave the names to Adam and Eve and mankind. God has dominion over us and cares for us perfectly. As God cares for us we have failed in the whole chain of dominion if we do not respect the dominion

God has for us, and give to God all the praise and all the glory that He deserves. We need to declare "Our Father who art in heaven, **hallowed** by they name."

The past? I did say there was a personal historical connection. In the 14th century an ancester of mine in northern Ireland was a mercenary. In this respect he did some work for the Lord of the Isles of that time. He clearly impressed the Lord of the Isles so much that he was given a large portion of land that equates with what is now the parish of Kildalton and Oa. A document related to this is held in Edinburgh and a copy of the document can be found in a book held in the Islay Museum. The surname of the ancestor was McVicar, which through the years the family name has evolved to what is now Magee. Through the centuries the land must have been sold many times of course but it seemed like a connection was there for me. The island of Islay was my first ministry and I recalled how at home I felt when arriving on the island for the first time. Could it be that historically there was this connection, some may ask. However, there is a more important reason. Whatever may happen on a human level as a Minister it is the spiritual level that counts, as can be seen in the second chapter of this book. It is the call of God that is most important, to feel that God has given a gift of a call and to settle into the gift of God. It is important always to sense that common bond with the people and our God as we seek to move together establishing the vision of the Lord.

Part 3
Reaching the unreachable

Harry loved the opportunity to be alone. This was nothing new for him. Long before I met with Harry. He was fostered to a crofting family as a youngster before the second World

War. Donald was the Baptist Minister on Islay just after the war and had a very successful ministry. During my time on the island many would look back on his time as being a golden era of Baptist ministry on the island. He would lead monthly "Kitchen Services" in the outlying farms and crofts, which gave the opportunity for those living in remote parts to be able to be a part of corporate fellowship. Donald noticed that he had not seen Harry at the service for a while and was deeply concerned about him. Harry loved to be out in the countryside and so was not easy to track down. However, one day Donald met Harry walking across the heather. Harry was caught. There was no way of getting away. Looking for a way to escape, Harry says "I cannot stop, Minister, I am just looking for a lost sheep." Donald was not slow in his reply, "So am I Harry, and I have found him."

The decades had passed, and Harry seemed to have disappeared. Some even wondered if he was still living. But Harry was still there, albeit an older man by this time, enjoying the solitude of life on the croft, till the time he fell ill. Despite all of his protests Harry was taken into hospital, which is where I first met up with him. There was no heather for Harry to walk over, no lost sheep to find, just a hospital bed to lie on as I visited him and befriended him. Harry was not happy being in hospital, this was not his home, he wanted his freedom as he saw it even if he was not fit to make his way across the hill side. Through time and a number of visits the barriers began to be broken down. He would often speak of his home that he loved. He reminisced about his past experiences, recalling his youthful times out with the sheep, appreciating the gentle breeze blowing through the air. This was the ideal for him, what he missed so much.

The time came when Harry was to be discharged. Before

leaving I told Harry how much I appreciated his stories from the croft and how I would love to see the croft for myself. Harry was silent for a while, perhaps pondering over his reply, and then saying that he would appreciate that too. The ice had been broken and a door was opened.

Visiting Harry was an interesting yet enjoyable experience. I found his home and had many a time sat around his fireplace each week. I learnt that at certain times of the year it was essential to have a pair of wellington boots in the back of the car. I would park the car on the road side, put on my boots, and walk up the long drive. Did I say "drive"? There were times when the "drive" was more like a river, hence the importance of the wellington boots. I would wade my way up the stream of water till I reached the door. Harry welcomed me in and then boiled the water on the fire range and made a cup of tea. There was no gas or electricity of any kind in the building and we would sit talking in a very dark room. There was a lack of all the modern facilities that we would consider to be essential. Some would say that Harry would have a better life if he came into town and lived in the Even tide Home, but for Harry there was nothing like the croft, that was his home. In our manner of relating to people it is important that we understand what is essential from their perspective and not just our own. If we want to be respected for our pastoral relationships then we have failed if our stock answer is that is how I see it, or that is just how I am. The important question is how they are and what makes them feel comfortable. In the same way we have failed if we say we are a touchy feeling character and hugs are normal to me. What is normal for the person we hug is more important. I know that for some people a hug can be a means of comfort, but it is not always appropriate. As a kind of compromise, when I shake hands I will grip the person's hand with my two hands.

It is less formal doing that, but is also avoiding any possibility of anything inappropriate.

You cannot hope to be understood until you are willing to do the same for others. The Bible says, "A person who answers without listening is foolish and disgraceful" (Proverbs chapter 18 verse 13). We are often so busy trying to get people to see it our way that we don't stop to listen to what they are saying.

Part 4
Mary

As a Pastor I am aware of some wonderful lessons that we can learn in visitation. Lessons are not merely to be learned in the study, but wherever we may go.

Mary lived on a remote farm some distance away. She had a deep love of her Lord but being in such a remote part was unable to join in fellowship with other believers. I have tended to give priority to pastoral visits of those who live a distance away. They often have the greatest need for fellowship compared to those living in the town or near the rest of the fellowship. Many times we had some interesting spiritual conversations as we shared coffee together. Sometimes I was the one that needed to discover spiritual truths in the visit. Mary kept an immaculate house, all neat and tidy, a place for everything and everything had a place. Yet she made room for me in her living room. However, as I came to visit in the spring I discovered I was not the only one that Mary made room for. As I was welcomed in I discovered that Mary had guests, two small lambs, running freely in her well organized living room. The living room was special to her, but the lambs were even more important. She explained to me that this is quite a common thing in the spring. The lambs had become orphans at birth. Mary was effectively the surrogate mother providing all the tender loving care that was needed. Without her the lambs would not have survived. She would feed the lambs using a baby's bottle and milk. She did everything she could until the time would come that the lambs were strong enough to go out and fend for themselves.

As I observed I was reminded of the shepherds of the bible. Jesus gave a parable that spoke of the shepherd that cares for the sheep. If one was lost nothing matters except to find the sheep and care for it. The shepherd may be tired and in need of a rest but for him it was more important that he cares for his lost sheep, giving it the best care that is possible. In the same way the psalmist, David, was a shepherd before he became a King. Even as a king he never forgot his roots and applied it to the relationship he had with God, the Good Shepherd. So he penned that well known psalm, "The Lord is my Shepherd, I shall not want". Mary did a grand job caring for those lambs, but how much more is the care that the Good Shepherd, our Lord and God, gives to you and I.

Part 5
Compassion Regardless

When visiting the local hospital on Islay I made it a practice to walk around after visiting the member of the church. It was a small cottage hospital so it was not a hard task to give time to all the patients that were there. On one occasion there was one patient I immediately recognised. She was the only person on the island, as far as I knew, who was a Jehovah Witness. She normally lived in Port Ellen, the main port for the ferry.

Jehovah's Witnesses are a people of a faith that many of us likely don't know much about. We may remember them as the people who often come to our homes to evangelize, but do we actually know what they believe? I am not going to spend time here to talk about their beliefs though I would say that there are a number of ways in which they differ from main stream Christianity. So I do not agree with them and do not commend them in any way, but as Christians we have been called to love all including those we disagree with you. Jesus said "My command is this: Love each other as I have loved you." (John chapter 15 verse 12)

As I came to her bedside I could sense a measure of nervousness, but I approached her and spoke with her as a friend. She looked at me and asked if I knew who she was. Of course I did. I had met her in Port Ellen with another Jehovah Witness who was visiting the island. We had talked about what the Bible says and discussed how we may differ. She could not understand why I would give time to visit her in hospital when she was a Jehovah Witness. I knew all of what she stood for, but Christian love is not restricted just to those in agreement. Indeed we are even exhorted to love our enemies.

I guess that comes back to what I spoke of before about being prepared to come out of our comfort zone. We cannot adequately speak of the God of love if we are not prepared to show that love even to those that seek to challenge us in our lives and beliefs.

Part 6
Genuine care

I recall visiting door to door in the Edinburgh area on one occasion. To be precise it was on the outskirts of the city. I was having a great day, enjoying the visits and spent a long time visiting one particular house. We spoke for some time and as the conversation came to an end the lady of the house asked me if I planned to visit her next door neighbour. I acknowledged that I was indeed planning to visit her next door neighbour. She advised me that the neighbour was elderly so wait a while as she does not move very fast. She also has very poor hearing so remember to knock very loudly. I was impressed that she cared so much for her neighbour that she made sure she did not miss out on a visit.

I went next door and knocked loudly. I waited, and I waited. Clearly she was right about her neighbour, I thought, the elderly neighbour was taking for ever. I knocked again, and still she did not come. It was at this point that a car pulled up. The driver wound the window down and called across to me, "Are you looking for Miss Jones?" I agreed that I was indeed looking for her, when he then gave to me an answer I never expected. "You will be a long time waiting, she died 3 months ago." That was a shock. The lady who I thought was so good for her neighbour did not really know her. I thought she was so supportive but she did not even know that the neighbour was dead and buried 3 months previously. She was a neighbour but did not really know her. To be caring we need to be able to demonstrate more about how we interact with people.

What does the Bible say about helping others? Quite a lot, actually! Both the Old and New Testament are filled with Bible verses about helping others in need. Serving others is clearly important in the eyes of God, but finding ways to serve can often fall by the wayside in our busy day to day lives. When we are too busy to know others we are too busy to care. The Good Samaratan was a busy man, but he had time to care for someone in need. Paul wrote "Carry each other's burdens, and in this way you will fulfill the law of Christ." (Galations chapter 6 verse 2) We were never meant to do life alone. We need the love and care of others, as much as we are needed by others in the same ways.

Part 7
God turned it into good

There will always be times when we wonder how we can cope in tough times. I know that from personal experience. The story I am about to share I have decided not to reveal any names nor details of the church involved or anything that would identify the central character. I am sure that for some the pain and heartache will still be there and I have no wish to cause any further pain. However, it is a true story and reveals how God will often be working in the background when we think there is no hope.

I still remember the day when a lady approached me in deep distress. It must have been her worst nightmare as she said her husband had gone to work that morning and not returned. It was long past the time when he should be home from work but there was no sign of him. I agreed to give her a lift and we made our way to his place of work. Things seemed so bad, but for this young lady it was about to get worse. When making enquiries the employer said, "But he no longer works here. He gave in his notice and said he was leaving." He had left her! The penny was beginning to drop. Soon we were to discover that he was not the only one who had left. A teenage girl about the same age as their son had also left. Secretly they had been having an affair and had been planning to run away together for some time. In addition, he was a man who had a leading role as a lay person in the local church.

I spent time seeking to console the deserted wife and to counsel her. The next step was to seek to support a church that was feeling overwhelmed with the whole situation. The church was the talk of the town, but for all the wrong reasons. The church members were concerned about how this would effect the witness and testimony of the church. Their heart had been to speak about how the grace of God changes people for the better, but this incident seemed to over shadow all of that. As a church it was decided that there was only one answer to this conundrum, prayer! That was the answer, talk to God about it and allow Him to deal with it because we can never sort things out.

God answered prayer so miraculously. It was as if he knew our need before we did and was already working on the answer. A young man from the community had gone to America with hopes for his future in a worldly sense but whilst there he discovered his spiritual future. Whilst in America he committed his life to Christ and was born again, as Jesus expressed it in John chapter 3. As he returned to his native community the gossip had turned from the negative to the positive. People could not understand the positive change in his life. A mini revival began to evolve as others turned from the past and commit themselve in faith to the God of love. It seemed to be bad, but God had turned it into good.

I recall someone who held an important role in the community asking me what I thought about these people that were calling themselves "Born Again Christians" as if he saw them as some strange cult. I was able to explain that this was actually part of main stream Christianity which is clearly marked out for us in the bible. He could not understand, but the one thing I knew was that what seeme to be bad, God had turned it into something good.

Chapter 12

Lock Down or Break Out?

The year is 2020! How can anyone forget the year of the Covid-19 pandemic, otherwise known as the Coronavirus pandemic. It was first detected in Wuhan, in China, in December 2019 but became worldwide early in 2020. In March 2020, the pandemic closed in like a fog, ushering in a strange new vocabulary, alarming statistics and the fear of illness and death. In the days before the first national lockdown was ordered, the government's chief scientific adviser suggested that a "good outcome" would be keeping UK deaths below 20,000, a number that sounded improbably awful at the time, but which has been dwarfed by the 233,791 deaths recorded as of December 2023. So, in March 2020 churches throughout the country were facing the issues relating to what was to be known as "the lockdown."

Part 1
Finance

An almost total ban on social gatherings was imposed during full national lockdowns. Household mixing rules were imposed to prevent people who do not live together from meeting. Sometimes these rules specified places (usually indoor spaces) where people could not meet. The rules prohibited anyone coming within two metres (6 foot 6 inches) of each other. For the churches to function adequately there was a need to discover new ways of doing church. As a result of the lockdowns there were some churches that closed permanently due to the financial implications and Ministers that were made redundant. For many churches the main source of income was from the offerings during Sunday services and/or rent received from those hiring halls. During the lockdown none of these opportunities were available. Nationally it seemed like the church was in retreat but does it need to be? In the church where I was ministering during this time, Perry Baptist Church, we have a very understanding membership who recognised that the bills for the church would continue to come in despite the building being closed, so they made sure that other arrangements were made to contribute financially. Either they would post cash to the Treasurer or they made an arrangement with the bank.

Part 2
Fellowship

However, church is about more than money. It is about fellowship under the headship of Christ. If the buildings are closed how is that possible? We needed to remind ourselves that despite how our culture may see things, church is not about buildings but is about the gathered believers, the people. The church is a vibrant community of believers united by faith and love for Jesus Christ. Throughout the Bible, we find teachings and exhortations that guide and inspire the Church in its mission to proclaim the Gospel and make disciples. As believers, church attendance is of high importance. It is a place we can all come together to worship, be encouraged, and learn from God's words for spiritual growth. How do we put this all into practice when meeting together is not possible?

PART 3
Zoom

In Perry the people are very open to ideas and also to suggest ideas. There are methods that are possible which were not available a generation ago. Technology has opened doors that enabled a form of fellowship to exist. It is not a perfect answer because we ideally need to meet face to face. The COVID pandemic taught the world many lessons, one of them being that meeting virtually can go a long way towards bridging the gap of physical distance. As a church we took those lessons on board in various ways. We discovered what is known as "Zoom", a system used for conferences in the business world when colleagues could not meet face to face. Using zoom we continued to hold weekly prayer meetings. This was our priority. Charles Spurgeon described the prayer meeting as being the powerhouse of the church. He was right and we were living in an age where we needed that power as the devil sought to divide us into small fragments. Secondly, using zoom we held weekly bible studies. Together the church had the means of teaching and learning what God's word has to say for today.

What about informal fellowship? What about the opportunity to interact with each other and to provide pastoral support? The church met that need in three ways. First of all we held weekly virtual coffee mornings using zoom. Clearly we each had to provide our own coffee but we provided mutual support and interaction with each other. It is a part of being human that we need these kinds of times together. Secondly, the members and adherents were all given telephone calls every week from the church leadership. This personal contact is important if we were to understand where they all are emotionally as well as spiritually and where we needed to counsel those in need. Thirdly, there were times when we could take a walk as long as we kept 2 metres away from each other. That may seem strange when used to communicating at a closer distance, but once again such a walk provided the chance of human interaction.

Part 4
YouTube

With the use of technology Sunday worship could also continue albeit in a different form. It was my own opinion that the Sunday worship would best be served by using the Youtube platform. At the time I was aware that I had my own health concerns and by using Youtube I could record in advance and if I could not be present at any given time then anyone could press the button and set everything in motion. In addition YouTube has an option to schedule any video in advance. However, there were other advantages. YouTube is a popular video creation and sharing social media platform, which is owned by Google. YouTube is also the world's second most used search engine after Google. This means that people use YouTube to search for information. It also means that video content on YouTube can easily be found on search engines. YouTube is different to other major social media platforms because its focus is solely about watching, creating, and engaging with video content. You can only post video content to YouTube. Because YouTube's sole focus is video content, finding your way around the platform is relatively straightforward. There is no need for viewers to obtain a password as is the case with Zoom, so it is easily accessed by those searching for services just as people in "normal" times can walk into a church straight off the street with freedom. This proved to be a great source of encouragement as the numbers provided by YouTube indicated that we were reaching more people than would fit into the building. Clearly this was filling a need. We decided to continue to use YouTube when the pandemic was over. It was not to be an alternative to face to face meetings but an additional means of reaching out to the world surrounding us. The lockdown became the inspiration for a small church to reach out beyond the walls of the building. As the church buildings opened up it is true to say the numbers went down because people could find live fellowship but the numbers that continued was sufficient for the church to feel God was doing something important through this medium. Since this form of ministry has begun we have learnt that there is more that can be done. Hashtags are a quick and easy means of 'categorising' our videos by tagging it with words or terms that best describe the subject matter. The most important function of a hashtag is to improve the video's 'searchability' because they tell YouTube specifically what the video is about so that they can be included in search results for those terms or phrases.

Building on this ministry the church experimented with a video advent calendar in December 2023. Each day of Advent there would be a different video. The plan was that it would be a short video from a different part of the locality with a message that Christmas is coming celebrating the birth of Jesus Christ. It was a success interms of the numbers of viewers and also in terms of a request from the community to do something similar for Easter. So the "Count down to the Resurrection" was born. One of these videos was to result in over 2,300 views, a magnificent result for such a small church.

Part 5
Radio

Radio was another medium that God has used to open up the avenues of communication even when the nation is under lockdown rules. Through the years I have been interviewed on radio as an author both in the UK and also abroad. In March 2020 I was interviewed by the late Ernie Almond on Black Cat Radio, the local radio for St. Neots. The interview was carried out by telephone due to the pandemic rules. After the interview Ernie mentioned that some of the clergy in St. Neots had formed a team to present a weekly Christian Sunday morning show, would I be interested in taking part? The idea was that the Clergy would be on a rota ensuring that despite the pandemic the community had an opportunity of hearing Christian music and a word for the week. Perry is a small rural village, so the chance of being a regular part of what was happening along with the wider community was amazing. I agreed and Ernie made contact with the leader of the team. Those in St. Neots had seen this as a vision they could all identify with providing a Christian resource for the community, and even in Perry this was something that the local people could hear. Here was another means of using technology to overcome the restrictions of the pandemic but the radio broadcasts still continue. It was as if God used the pandemic as a tactical retreat in our spiritual battles. Irrespective of what time the radio station may give to us this was a bonus. I continue to meet people in various places who have spoken of hearing the good news of the Saviour as they tuned into "Black Cat Radio". The Lord opened up the door of opportunity, may we never be the ones to close the door God has opened up. The devil thought he had closed down churches but God had other ideas asthe gospel was advanced.

Part 6
The return

The church needed to prepare for the return to the church building as the lockdown came to the end. God had certainly enabled us to function in a new way but our Lord never intended us to continue in that way. We need to look to ways in which we can interact with people more fully once again. We needed to ensure that the chairs were adequately spaced out, we needed to be familiar with all the rules on sanitation but on that aspect we were aware that books cannot be used. So, when it comes to Sunday worship what is going to happen with regard to hymns and the following of the Bible readings. Initially we were to listen to hymns but how do we read what we are listening to? The date was announced when we were permitted back into the church as a congregation. The maintenance team set to work in placing a large television screen on the wall at the front of the church. The purpose of the television screen was to have the words of hymns and the bible reading displayed and easily read without breaking the law. At this point I would be amiss if I did not mention the late Miss Iris Mumford who left a legacy for the church which funded the purchase of the screen. Thank you Iris for remembering the church and being willing to be used by the Lord in this way.

Beyond the time of the pandemic the screen continues to be useful in God's work for other reasons. When the congregation sings from a book the singing will go down into the book and therefore not be so audible. When the congregation sings from looking up at a screen the sound will go out and therefore enhances the worship. The devil thought he was bringing the church down with the pandemic, yet in reality, God was raising His people up.

As a Pastor I would like to acknowledge those who played their part during this difficult time. Thank you to the Deacons for their leadership as they pooled together ideas that would bring the church through a difficult time. Thank you to the members and adherents of the church who were open to new ideas that have moved the church forward. Most importantly, thank you God for the most important support of all, thank you Lord for your support, encouragement and strength when we were at our most vulnerable point in life.

It seemed like a long time since the pandemic began. For many, this has been the most challenging time in their lives. Sickness, lockdowns and arguably worst of all—fear—have run rampant around the globe for such a long time. The impact on mental health has probably been the most overlooked aspect of COVID. And we haven't even touched on the difficulties people face whether there's a pandemic or not. Yet, we are not alone. God is with us and His Word speaks life into our challenges. Even when times get tough, we still have One we can depend on to give us strength. God cares A LOT about getting us through hard times. The Psalmist says in Psalm 46 verse 1 "God is our refuge and strength, a very present help in trouble."

Chapter 13

Come together

I am recalling a time when I served in the Midlands. It struck me how close some churches were geographically. There were four Baptist churches that were literally within walking distance of each other. Three of them were in the Baptist Union and one was not. Looking through the local history it would appear that during the past couple of centuries the churches each in turn had a fall out and those that split from the church established a new church a short walk away. No matter how important our forefathers saw the principles they made a stand on the reality is that the world looks on and envisages a divided Christian community. Our divisions can never be beneficial to the Christian witness in any given community, indeed it is quite the opposite. As I see a situation such as this it is important for all of us to find a way in which we can move forward together. We need to focus on the words of Jesus who said "By this shall all men know that you are my disciples, that you have love one for another." On the long term I am not so sure that I have been successful as I would like to be, but as they say "nothing ventured nothing gained". An attempt needed to be made.

Of the three union churches there were two churches that had Ministers serving locally. One of the first things I did was to find the other local minister and introduce myself to him. Paul and his wife Joanne made me welcome as we fellowshipped together. We soon discovered that we had something in common with each other, a love of Jesus. What a great ideal to be able to share, more important than the principles of division that had been featured so much through the centuries. Here was something worth building on as a healthy Christian relationship is established. Paul and Joanne, thank you for your friendship.

My own wife, Joan, and I met regularly with Paul and Joanne, along with another Minister and his wife from a church a few miles away. The other Minister was Adrian Lloyd and his wife, Cath. We prayed together, we encouraged each other, we shared in the joys as well as the sorrows of life. Ministry can sometimes be a lonely journey and we need times such as this as we seek to plough through all that lies before us. I really valued this fellowship together. When we were later to move both these Ministers were invited to take part in the transition. Paul led the farewell meeting and spoke. Adrian was to speak at the induction service at my next church.

It was Paul that made the next suggestion on our journey together. The fellowship we are sharing as Ministers is wonderful, but what about our people? Is this the time when we can draw them into this interchurch fellowship? Perhaps once a month meeting together, praying together. To move forward we need to be praying for each other. There was a third union church that did not have a minister, why not include them as we meet. And so we did. For the first time these three union churches were getting together. Not all the members of all the churches were meeting, but enough to fill a fair sized room, which was encouraging. My hope is that at some point this is something that would resume long term as the church's witness to the community about the love of God.

As a partnership of churches grew so came the opportunity to support each other in practical ways. Sometimes our own church would have gospel concerts with well known singers. A great opportunity, but we lacked the sound equipment that would be needed in such a situation. The neighbouring church, New Hope, had the equipment and the expertise to put it all together. Working together God will do mighty things in all of us. When Paul was away our churches were close enough for me to dash across when our morning service was complete and bring a sermon for them too. When any of the churches had something special on we were able to try and support each other for the glory of God. Their time of Worship was contemporary and vibrant, with a full band leading the congregation into praising God and lifting their voices to Him. It was a joy to share with them in this way.

The Baptists were not the only denomination in the locality. There were also the Methodist and the Anglican churches. I wanted to build bridges with each of them, though perhaps this happened more naturally and more effectively with the Methodist church. That may be a more natural step for me as prior to my call into Baptist Ministry I was a Methodist Local Preacher, or a lay preacher, as can be seen in chapter 2 of this book. My theology may have changed but that should not deter from extending a hand of friendship and Christian love. Methodism, whose origins, doctrine and practice derive from the life and teachings of John Wesley. George Whitefield and John's brother Charles Wesley were also significant early leaders in the movement. They were named Methodists for "the methodical way in which they carried out their Christian faith". Methodism originated as a revival movement within Anglicanism originating out of the Church of England in the

18th century and became a separate denomination after John Wesley's death.

The nearest Methodist church to us was Upper Ettingshall Methodist Church. It was known locally as "Sodom Chapel" from the biblical town where Lot and his family lived for a time. Upper Ettingshall road, where the church is situated, was initially known by the name of Sodom road due to the character of those living in the area in previous centuries being a reminder of the evil that existed in the biblical Sodom though I would not describe the present residents in such a way as that. In earlier centuries that I am refering to the men worked hard down the mines or in nail shops. After work they would go to the pub or drink their own home brew, get drunk, and end up in fights or other forms of trouble. Some may wonder why a church would be happy being known by such a nickname. However, here is a reminder of the grace of our Lord that God can raise each of us up out of our past and give to us a better future in the love of God.

So what about the present day? Joan and I visited the church one Tuesday morning. They held a regular community cafe on the premises. This was their way of reaching out and engaging with the community that surrounded them. Community cafés are run by volunteers and offer reasonably priced refreshments and a warm welcome to everyone. They exist to keep people connected rather than to make a profit.

This cafe also provided breakfast. This was the beginning of wonderful friendships as we shared together our hopes for both the present and the future. They were a small fellowship, but a fellowship that worked hard as they engaged with those that surrounded them. Not sure that we did a lot in practical terms, but we did seek to encourage them with our presence at some of the various events that took place on the premises.

Unity is a common topic in the Bible, promoting the peacefulness of living unified in harmony. We are called by the Bible to be in unity within ourselves, in unity with all followers of Jesus, and maintain the unity of the Spirit. The Bible emphasizes the importance of unity among believers and within the body of Christ. The psalmist said "How good and pleasant it is when God's people live together in unity!" (Psalm 133 verse 1) May we collectively look to the ways in which we might encourage a unity.

Chapter 14

Expect the unexpected

Part 1
The unexpected flowers

Life is not always as it seems. In ministry it is important to be careful and ensure that we do not jump to the wrong conclusions. I recall a gentleman that I had a huge respect for. We had many conversations together with him and his wife. We talked together, we prayed together, we shared together our past experiences and our future hopes. The time came, however, when my friend went to be with the Lord and I officiated at his funeral. There were many wonderful words and tributes that were given by the people that knew him, and he had a wonderful send off. Clearly he was a man well respected by those that shared his journey of life.

It was a shock, however, when an unusual package came through the post. It was a flower sent by a lady from another district and with the flower came some very flowery and poetical writing that spoke of a romantic connection she knew with the deceased. There was another letter addressed to myself requesting that the package be placed at the last resting place of my friend. I could sense the commotion that would have soon emerged if anyone had seen such a sight at his last resting place. It would have been a denial of all the wonderful words that were said about him. What anquish would have been felt by his family, the hurt that would have broken their hearts even more than they already knew! What was I to do? The answer was simple as I saw it. I had made no promises to deliver any packages from anyone. I slipped outside and gave the package a respectful "funeral" as I buried it in the dustbin. Whatever may have been the thoughts of this lady it was not worth causing further distress to anyone, and I told no one about the package from that day till now. Times such as these are times of discretion, and thats just the way that I applied it.

In fairness to my dear friend, he and his wife had previously told me of the difficulties they had had from a young lady in a district where they had previously lived. The lady had some mental health issues and had imagined there was a relationship with my friend that did not exist, and it was not mutually shared. As a couple he and his wife had sought to help and support her but as they discovered how she was thinking they decided to take a step back till they moved away. That maybe a lesson for all in ministry, be careful how we deal with sensitive information such as this.

Part 2

The bomb!

How on earth does a minister end up in a bomb plot? Yet it happened to me!

It was election day. I stopped outside the local polling station which was often held in the Bowmore Hall on Islay. I carried out the business of my civic responsibility which I had called there for. It was not far from where I lived but I had other matters to attend to and wanted to have the car available for a quick get away. The quick get away, as I saw it, was not going to happen. I put the key into the ignition and turned the key hoping for a good response. Nothing happened! I tried again, still no joy. I clearly had a problem. Ministers cannot always afford reliable cars, as my experiences often showed. I guess that was the end of my hopes of getting to my next appointment.

It was at this point that I saw my friend John. I was confident he was the answer to my predicament. He was employed to drive lorries all round the island so he would have the experience to help. I spoke with John and asked if he could help with some jump leads attached to the battery. He agreed and the leads were attached between my car and his lorry. Right, we are now ready to start, I thought. Nothing could go wrong now, surely. I sat in the driving seat turned the ignition, and to my horror heard an enormous "Boom!". The noise was deafening.

It would appear that there was an excess of fumes on my battery and as I turned the ignition it set off the explosion. What a mess from one battery, in more ways than we could imagine. This was not the end of the matter, as if it couldn't get any worse. The news soon took a trip all round the island as people asked each other "Did you hear that someone tried to blow up the polling station at the Bowmore?" It seems like a reasonable question to ask. It was only twenty miles across to northern Ireland and it would have been easy for the IRA to access the island of Islay. Chinese whispers had taken on a mind of its own. If you ever hear of a Baptist Minister being involved in a bombing plot I will certainly deny it. Trust me, things are not always as they seem.

Part 3
Hearse driving

I could not believe my eyes. This has to be the most unusual experience I have known during my ministry. As I walked down the street there was a hearse coming down the hill, with no driver at the wheel. Like many other Ministers I would often have seen such a vehicle, but never being driven with no driver. The name hearse is historically derived from the French, but today the word hearse is only ever used to describe vehicles that have been specially adapted to carry coffins – generally they are big, shiny, black cars with an extended chassis and large windows to display the coffin from all angles. It is unlikely that I would miss seeing a driver in such a vehicle, but he was not there.

The hearse had been delivered to a nearby garage for servicing, and subsequently left parked on the road outside the garage, at the top of the hill. I have no idea whether there was a fault with the brakes or if the hand brake had accidentally been left off, but either way the car was not secured in a parking position. It seemed like it was all happening in slow motion as the vehicle began moving diagonally across the road and eventually coming to rest in a lamp post on the corner of the street. It was a major road in the town, and to this day I am amazed that the vehicle did not pick up any passengers on the way. Fortunately there were no casualties resulting from the incident. Quickly a number of us were gathered around seeking to find a way of dealing with the need. Put simply the hearse needed to be pushed back to a more appropriate place. Then in their wisdom decided that if we all pushed then there would be no direction given, then turned to me and said that I was needed to sit in the driving street and steer. I agreed and got in behind the wheel. It was only then that I realised how weird this must seem for any looking on, a minister complete with clerical collar appearing to be driving the hearse. However, it was too late, I was there and needed to get on with the job assigned to me.

I guess there is a moral there. Whether we see it as being weird or not team work requires us to apply ourselves to the role that has been given to us. Life at its best is just like that.

Chapter 15

Partnership Missions

Partnership missions are a great concept of churches partnering, or sharing, together for the sake of the gospel, the good news of the Saviour. The hope and expectation is it will be an authentic expression of our reality as churches become partners in mission. It's a wonderful journey that helps churches discover a sense of purpose, discern the call of God, and engage in joyful, hopeful mission in their local communities. It is a partnership of Christians and churches who through working together seek to serve and support the local Church in making Jesus known. Scripturally there are many examples of the importance of Christians and fellowships working together. My involvement with such missions in the churches where I was the Pastor has predominantly been with American churches though I am aware that churches have successfully conducted partnership missions with churches from other countries. I was conscious that if we had a team of Americans conducting traditional door to door visitations would not be helpful in a British community. There was a real risk that when hearing an American accent at the door that there would be an assumption that it must be a team of Mormons, which would not be helpful to the local Baptist church in the UK. Clearly that is not the fault of the team, that was their natural tongue. However, with a touch of wisdom it is possible to make use of culture positively for the sake of the gospel. I have, as a Pastor, hosted a large number of American partnership teams and the vast majority of the teams accepted that we would not be using them for door to door visitation. The exception was just two people on one team who decided they would ignore advice given and decided they would operate in a way that was more appropriate in their American culture rather than the British culture that the team were working in. In such a situation the local Pastor is the one that is then left to pick up the pieces seeking to carry out the long term work of the locality. None of them were in the teams that I may mention in this chapter. What I would say is that for a partnership of this nature to work the teams need to listen to the guidance of the hosts who know the culture best.

I am so pleased that with that exception the teams were wonderful as they worked hard to partner with us. Rev. David Drake was the leader of a team that came to us in Islay, in the Hebrides, in the 1980's. At the time he was the Pastor of a church in Florida but before retiring recently was the Association Mission Strategist at Northeast Florida Baptist Association. I asked him recently for his thoughts as he reflected on his visit with us in Scotland. He said that for him "It was a life experience I'll never forget. It was very well planned for our arrival. You pastored multiple churches but focused on using the team in the appropriate area. Praise God for a few who gave their lives to Jesus." Thank you David for your kind words.

We need to remember that the hopes of a mission are not dependant just on the period when our international visitors are with us. The partnership continues as the local church continues with what has been started. The mission can be an opportunity to draw together folks we may not normally be able to reach, but having made the contact we as a local church need to continue the work of demonstrating the love of God and fulfilling the spiritual needs of the community. What did we do when seeking to make a positive input drawing two cultures together as we seek to present the good news of the Saviour? As I said before, one has to use wisdom, but in doing so a church and its team will reach more people from the community than might be the case with traditional evangelism. In the evenings we were able to put on theme nights that could draw the interest of others. One evening would be a "Scottish evening", remembering that the partnership missions I was involved in were held in Scotland. Such an idea can be adapted to other parts of the UK focusing in the local culture or types of food from the area of the church. Such an evening of a Scottish night would include the local food, such as haggis and other Scottish delicacies. Haggis is not too appealing to the taste buds from America but I am so proud of our American friends that gave it a try. Musically we might have a piper to play the bagpipes, or a demonstration of Scottish country dancing. People love to be able to show the international visitors the culture they have grown up with. In the midst of that will always come the opportunity for the visitors to explain the reason they have come as they speak of the love of God and share a testimony. Another evening may be an "American Night". Like the Scottish night it is an opportunity to hear of the culture of our guests, but in that framework we hear how the Lord Jesus burst into the scene and provided something even better. A welcome meal always goes down well, remembering to invite local celebrities and political leaders. That gives a good start to the week. The possibilities are endless.

Through the day time schools often appreciate the opportunity to bring people from other cultures into the school from an educational perspective, especially if it is in a rural setting away from the big city. There is also the traditional opportunity of the school assembly, but remembering that within the school setting proselyting is not permitted. There can, however, be children's meetings or youth events held at the church where young people can meet the special guests of the week.

I have also found that adult groups and organisations have appreciated the opportunity to partner with us. We would send no more than two members of the team to any given group that agreed to them coming. Local businesses were also pleased to invite folks from abroad to come and see whatever maybe the work that they do. It all adds to the public relations of the church in its long term desire to share the love of God in its community. Members of the church might also invite members of the team to afternoon tea, or a coffee morning, in their homes along with their friends and neighbours. The ideas can be numerous, but a little imagination and thought is important.

How did the teams see these visits to Scotland? Rev Don Satterwhite, who led one team to us in Fife, recently shared some of his reflections of his trip to Scotland with the following words, "The mission trip to Lochgelly, Scotland, was a wonderful and eye opening experience for five believers from the New England city of Litchfield, CT. While I had been to Lochgelly before my wife and three other ladies from our church made the trip. We enjoyed interacting with people from both the church and community. I had the privilege of speaking in several services at the Lochgelly Baptist Church. One evening was an American night with hot dogs and hamburgers. They were not able to find hamburger buns but we made do with rolls. That was the biggest crowd of the week. We also were able to meet with community groups and spoke in the public schools as well. Politics was a topic of interest as Barack Obama was running for president." Once again, thank you for your kind words Don.

What surprised me was to discover how the partnership missions also had an impact on the ongoing ministry of some when they returned to America. Michael Hilliard led a team that came to us in Fife in the year 2,000. Recently he shared how the visit made an impact upon his life. He said "I first visited Scotland twenty-four years ago as part of a ministry partnership between Baptists in Scotland and the United States. The experience was not only highly rewarding but also challenged my views of ministry which had a formative and lasting impact of how I view the Church's ministry in society and the world. My experience and education was that impact was to be through sharing the Gospel from the pulpit and through conversation (i.e. the Romans road, the four spiritual laws, etc.) which seemed to work in the Southern US. The partnership, and specifically Jon's ministry in the town of Lochgelly, challenged those deeply held beliefs of ministry. The partnership consisted of community engagement through meetings, conversations, and oh, so much tea and caffeine (which I do not mind) as the main point of connection with preaching and worship services being the second point. This focus was unique and novel to me and, I think, had greater impact upon the community than what my own philosophy of ministry would have provided. I remember so many conversations with different community leaders talking about the people of Lochgelly and the surrounding area, lamenting on the weather (☺), and our own spiritual experiences and journeys. These wonderful and rewarding experiences not only challenged my preconceptions and praxis of ministry but also helped me re-form the views I currently have of both church and ministry today." Michael, thank you for sharing these experiences from an early time of your ministry, So pleased that your experiences with us proved to be beneficial for your ongoing work for the Lord.

The team will be working hard, and a day of somewhere during this time is important. I do think that it is good to find something that would be unique for the team. We had a team at one point led by Rev Conley Shellander, Pastor of Monument Baptist Church, Grand Junction, Colorado that came to Islay in the Hebrides. Colorado is an American state that is land locked. What would be better for them than a visit to a light house? It would be a sight they would not normally be able to see. Add to that another factor, this lighthouse is surrounded by water, it could not be accessed without the availability of a boat. We gathered in Portnahaven waiting for the boatman to transport us over. He was full of interesting information as he spoke of his knowledge of island life as we boarded his boat. We all looked to him with admiration for all of that and because he was so willing to give his time for us. Later there were other thoughts that came to mind. We were half way over when the boatman turned to us and said "Do you realise that we are now in the midst of the most treacherous waters of the British Isles?" Now we wondered, why did he wait till we were half way over before telling us of the dangers of this crossing. He was right about the dangers. Nearby was a whirl pool which created the danger, and underneath were many wrecks that had fallen victim to the whirl pool. This does, of course, highlight the purpose of why these towers called lighthouses exist. Lighthouses mark dangerous coastlines, hazardous shoals, reefs, rocks, and not forgetting whirl pools, and safe entries to harbours. This was an experience that the team would never forget, though I am sure that Conley would in future years have found that this was a great sermon illustration, the importance of looking to the light to avoid the spiritual risks in life. Sadly I have lost contact with Conley, so cannot ask him for his reflections. I have heard that he has now retired somewhere in Texas.

Rev Don Satterwhite spoke of another way in which he spent his day off in a manner that fitted with his personal needs. He said "I was also able to travel to a village in the Lake District just below the border to experience my families roots in Sattherthwaite. The history of my family of Origin meant a great deal to me. Jon & Joan were so gracious a small group of Yankees. I hope that one day I'll be able to preach for Pastor Jon Magee in England." Clearly Don continues to have a heart for ministering in the United Kingdom as he would speak also of the most important kingdom, the Kingdom of God. Don, I am so pleased that your time with us proved to be beneficial in your personal family research as well as in sharing the gospel from your heart.

CHAPTER 16

Preaching in America

"My name in lights at Monument Baptist church, Grand Junction, Colorado"

It was during the 1980's and 1990's that I was to have the opportunity of a number of preaching tours. Twice I was to be in the state of Colorado, mostly at Grand Junction but also in

Denver. Once I was in Dallas, Texas. Twice I was in the state of Florida. One thing that struck me about America was the variety among the different states. For some in Britain there is a risk of speaking of something being "typical American". The reality is that there is no such thing as typical American. As one looks at the various states in America I was amazed at how different thay all are, whether that be culturally, geographically, economically or in any other way. Every state is different and the people are different too. Probably what we may see as being typically American is probably what Americans see as being typically Texan. In this chapter I plan to share a few experiences during my American tours. As one would expect, such tours were largely about preaching. Preaching on the Sunday all day with maybe youth events in between, and preaching each evening in various venues.It will also include being open to other forms of opportunity of sharing Gods love as the host church directs.

Part 1
Childs perspective

Before looking at other aspects I want to share a different perspective. The childrens view. On my first preaching tour I took my family with me as well as a young member of our church, Ruth, who was gifted musically and a good singer. For them it was an eye opener as they saw life in a new way. Sitting in a restaurant their eyes opened wide as they saw the police walk in, complete with guns in possession. We had not been in America long, just a day or two, and they discovered not every country has the same outlook on life. For our children this was new, never having seen any armed police in the United Kingdom. Guns are deeply ingrained in American society and the nation's political debates. The Second Amendment to the United States Constitution guarantees the right to bear arms, and about a third of U.S. adults say they personally own a gun. Guns are deeply ingrained in American society and the nation's political debates. So unlike us this was the norm for many.

In the UK we take a completely different stand on the issue of gun control. So with the contradicting outlooks on something so important how do we work together for the sake of the gospel? We have a lot to learn from children, perhaps more than the other way around. I have spoken of the shock the childen had seeing a completely different culture to our selves with regard to guns. Yet the same children were soon making friends with both the American children and also the adults. The reality is that if we want to share the love of God we need to demonstrate unconditional love for others, crossing the cultural divide. Well done to the children for leading the way on this important aspect of mission. In other matters of the trip, it is no wonder that the children were received well as they sang in front of the crowds.

Part 2
The corner where the devil hides!!

In addition to preaching in the evenings and through out the day on sundays there would also be visits to schools and nursing homes. The owner of a Supermarket also invited me to be a store chaplain for the day, spending time with customers as well as staff. I was given complete freedom not only to listen to them all as they shared their concerns but also to speak of the answers that are in the scriptures. There was no restrictions regarding anything I might say on spiritual matters. The owner of the store was prepared to make his business freely open to the presentation of the good news of the Saviour.

The school visits did have restrictions however. In the UK the schools teach Religious Education and have a regular religious assembly. American public schools however have a different position on religion in schools. This was not always the case, but there was a change that came about in the 1960's. A lot of people would attribute the change to a lady by the name of Madalyn Murray O'hair. She was an American activist supporting atheism, and separation of the church and state. In 1963, she founded American Atheists and served as its president until 1986, after which her son Jon Garth Murray succeeded her. She created the first issues of American Atheist Magazine and identified as a "militant feminist".

Madelyn Murray O'Hair is best known for a lawsuit, which challenged the policy of mandatory prayers and Bible reading in Baltimore public schools, in which she named her first son William J. Murray as plaintiff. She declared that this contravened her sons constitutional rights. Since then public schools have been so concerned in case they also were sued and as a consequence they ceased to have morning prayers or the teaching of anything religious in the school. If it was raised by a student it was permitted to respond with a religious answer but it was not permitted to overtly teach anything from the front. The irony is that the son she claimed to be concerned about was later to become a Christian and wrote his testimony in a book that was to become a best seller mainly because of who his mother was. According to the son his mother was far from caring in the family home.

So this is the reason why our presentation in the schools was different. Outside of the school it was about the presentation of faith. In the schools it was a presentation of our culture, an educational presentation. We needed to recognise that anything to do with faith could only be done in response to questions raised by the students, and surprisingly enough there were appropriate questions raised. Denominational schools, however, were clearly guided by a different set of rules.

Usually the hosts made arrangements directly with the schools themselves, but one church had a different approach and made contact with the Education Director for the area. An appointment was made for me to meet with her to discuss what I would be doing. I gathered together all the things I would take with me into the schools and prepared for the interview. As a preamble I asked two questions. The first question was, is it appropriate to say that I am here to speak about our culture though my work in the UK is about speaking about the love of God? The answer was a clear no. The second question I asked was whether it is appropriate to say that though I am speaking in other places about the love of God in the school I will be speaking about our culture. Once again the answer was no, the love of God must not be mentioned in any way. I accepted what she said, it is their premises and so we go by their rules. That is common courtesy. I began to show her the things I had brought with me. I showed her the Scottish tartan kilt, which the students were welcome to try on, then the peat which I had personally cut ready to heat up a fire place. These were things that the regular American student would not have seen before and was of benefit to their education. I had a whole variety of pictures that were also beneficial educationally. Then I showed her a picture of a church that was near where we lived. It was known as "the round church" and was built round. I explained that there was an interesting legend about the church, but I expect it is something I would not be allowed to talk about, I said. She took the bait as she asked "What is the legend?" The legend says that the church was built round so that there would be no corners for the devil to hide in, but inside all the pews are squared off. Guess where the corners are, where the people are. It is the people that the devil is interested in. I then added that I do not expect I could talk about that in the school. What a surprise when she said "yes, you can talk about that. That is quite acceptable". I could not believe what I was hearing. I could talk about the devil but do not mention that God loves you. Here is the message that the world is waiting to hear and is needing, God loves you!

Part 3
Opportunity

It was good to see the imagination that was used by some of my American hosts. One town had a skating rink that they were able to hire for the evening. It was explained to me that the management of the skating rink were happy for people to sponsor an evening. People could come in to skate as normal, but half way through the evening the sponsors had liberty to give a session promoting whatever they stood for. It was a fun evening but also a profitable one as the gospel was presented. I certainly enjoyed the skating, it was fun. I was also amazed at how willing the public were to listen to the gospel presentation. There was singing, which is always a good medium to share a message. Singing is not one of my talents but there were others in the team who could sing very well. One person spoke of how they came to faith. Then a Christian message from myself.

Then there was the use of the media. A time was agreed to meet with the local press. For them this was big news in the local scene, people coming across the Atlantic from Scotland, which is where we lived at that time. Coming not merely for a holiday but to partner with a church in their locality, visiting schools with the cultural presentation but also spending time both in the church and the community with a simple message. The message? "God loves you." It was headline news as they reported positively what was happening in their local church, and also the photographs taken which added something to the report.

I remember also the day I went into one of the schools to find a television crew were there filming. It never dawned on me at first what the reason was for the television crew being in the school. They filmed us as we each took time with our presentation, following us as we went from one session to another. Then I was invited into a room where they interviewed myself, asking the reason why we had come all this way for them, the people of America. Later that day we gathered around the television in someones home and saw the finished product. Through the use of the media the good news of the Saviour was brought to almost every home covered by the newspapers and the television. A local person commented that some spend their whole lives hoping to get on television, yet we were hardly in the country when the television crew came to us. How come that happened? The simple answer is that God opened the doors as he used people who were willing to use their imagination in the work of the Lord.

Part 4

Feeling the heat.

It was the middle of summer as I arrived in Florida, often known as the "Sunshine State". This trip it was going to be in the north west of Florida. Florida's Panhandle is renowned for outdoor adventure, family fun, and its stunningly white beaches. That all sounds great for a holiday, but it was more than a holiday for me. As I flew into Pensacola I was aware there was a busy schedule ahead. The diary would be full of preaching engagements, midweek bible teaching, speaking at breakfast and lunch meetings, youth meetings, visits to schools. There only seemed like one difficulty at the start of this tour, my luggage. I had arrived at Pensacola but my luggage had arrived at a completely different part of the country! I needed to return to the airport for my luggage before beginning my schedule, but eventually all was returned to the rightful owner of the luggage.

My first Sunday began well. It began with a sunday school class. In America, certainly in Baptist churches, it was the norm for the church to operate "all age education". Sunday school was not meant to be just for children as is usually the case in the UK. The Sunday School was a major feature for all ages. So at every church I visited my Sunday would begin with Sunday school before attending the main morning worship. This Sunday was planned in just the same way. All went well in the Sunday School and the Morning worship and the message was well received on both occassions. During the afternoon I met with the youth, unaware of the dangers that were awaiting me in the church building when I returned for the evening service. In America the preacher does not lead the worship. There is a Music Minister who is assigned to lead that part of the service, the preacher sits in the congregation till he is invited to come forward to bring the word of God. During the evening service all appeared to be well as the congregation sang their praises to God. All seemed to be well, until I came forward to preach. I opened my mouth, and no words came out. This was a new experience for me. I have no problem with public speaking, throwing my voice seems to come as a natural gift. So what has gone wrong this time?

Someone went out and fetched a glass of water but I did not need to drink any. As I held the glass in front of me my voice mysteriously returned. It was most bizarre. I could not understand what was happening, but with my voice now available I preached my heart away with glass in hand. That was the first time I preached with a glass in hand. I spoke with one of the church leadership who began apologising most profusely. He then began to explain the cause of my dilemma. They had felt sorry for the preacher who had joined them from Scotland. It was July, the middle of a very hot summer in Florida. How would this visiting preacher cope after a busy day in the heat. So, after some discussion they decided to leave the air conditioning on all day between the services so the preacher would find a cooler atmosphere in the evening service. What was not taken into account is that the air conditioning is not just about cooling the atmosphere, but it also removes the humidity from the air. Now it was all beginning to make sense. The glass held in hand was just sufficient to bring back some humidity and remove the dryness in my speech. Air conditioning is the process of removing heat from an enclosed space to achieve a more comfortable interior temperature and in some cases also strictly controlling the humidity of internal air. This time the humidity was certainly not controlled as it should be.

Part 5
Watch your language!

In our preaching we must always address the language of the listeners. We can preach some wonderful sermons but if the people do not understand the message we have wasted our time. There are a number of ways in which we can fail to reach people with the language that is being used. We need to recognise that for many coming to the church for the first time it will be like a culture shock. So much will be very different from what they are used to outside of the church. So the use of theological words maybe fine for the preacher, but not necessarily for the listener that may be hearing these words for the first time. There is no reason to expect them to understand. I recall a lecturer at the Bible Training Institute coming into the lecture hall, grabbing a piece of chalk, and writing for all to see "K.I.S.S." Kiss? That seemed like a strange message to send to the students. Then he explained that it meant "Keep It Simple Stupid", and rather than being a message to the students it was intended to be a reminder to himself. Keep it simple, and thats just when speaking with our native tongue to people with the same racial background.

That must surely be even more important when addressing people of a different racial background. I recall the time when my host said they had arranged for me to speak to Spanish speaking Mexicans at a Spanish mission. I had never spoken in Spanish before. The best I could do is to say "mañana", which means "tomorrow". I could never preach a whole sermon using just that one word. Realising my dilemma they immediately added, "Do not worry, we have an interpretter". Thats a good start, but it is not the full story. When talking through an interpretter it is important to have an understanding of his or her difficulties in the task of communicating faithfully the message they have heard. It is even more important to adhere to the reminder of the college lecturer, KISS, Keep It Simple Stupid". Forget the theological jargon, it will add to the complexity of the task of translating into a different language. Forget fast talking, give every opportunity of all the words being heard before it is being translated into another language. Give appropriate pause not too far into what you are saying, once again giving more opportunity for understanding and communicating the words into another language. It was using these principles that I sought to preach Gods word faithfully. It was a new experience for me and I confess to feeling very inadequate in the task. However, as we came to a close of the meeting three young men in this small mission declared that they wanted to begin a relationship with Jesus Christ, to turn from their past in repentance and discover Gods love for them. This was not about me the preacher, but it was a partnership with the interpretter undergirded by the power of the Holy Spirit. It was at this point that I left it to their own countrymen to counsel them in their own language as they began a new spiritual journey following the one who said "I am the way, the truth and the life." (John chapter 14 verse 6)

Part 6
Take time

My time in America involved a very heavy schedule. There was something happening each day whether it be in the morning, the afternoon or the evening. It was with wisdom that my hosts insisted in ensuring there was also time for me to relax. Without such times one would soon experience burn out. However, such times can also be opportunities of learning.

I remember the time when a young person decided it would be wonderful if I were to see an alligator in its natural environment. I was not so sure that this was a good idea as I visualised all the risks of meeting up with a hungry alligator. Despite my apprehension I agreed to go along with the idea and meet "Ally", the alligator. We got ready and set off on the adventure making our way to the swamp. My young friend assured me that he knew exactly where to go. We stood on a low bridge looking into the swamp. Swamp is a type of wetland ecosystem characterised by mineral soils with poor drainage and by plant life dominated by trees. The flow of water through wetlands is slow because of low gradients and retarding effects of the vegetation. Dead plant matter settles rather than being washed away. The slow replacement and lack of turbulence in the water result in a low rate of oxygen supply. Decay of the dead vegetation quickly uses up what ever oxygen is supplied, so that the mud and bottom waters are low or lacking in oxygen content. Under these conditions, the decay of organic matter is incomplete. This causes an accumulation of the more resistant fraction in the substratum. The familiar swamp water, varying from yellow to such a deep brown that it resembles strong tea or coffee, is the result. So here we were on the bridge looking down on a deep brown coloured swamp. Looking intently for the alligator and seeing nothing. The possible reason for that is the darkness of the environment making it impossible to see anything. These reptiles are kind of clumsy on land though they can still move fairly fast, but they're built for life in the water. Great swimmers, they are equipped with webbed feet and strong tails that propel them through the water. So this is the area we ought to see them but in the dark water they were not visible.

Suddenly the young person called "Look, look over there!" He was right, it was there in the swamp after all. It seemed so still, harmless even. What is there to fear? It was then that someone threw something in the water and I had to admit that I have never seen jaws moving so fast before. Yes, they are something to fear. Interestingly, I was told that alligators are usually frightened of adult humans though love children and dogs. But when tourists throw food to them in the hope of getting pictures it is at that point that they lose their fear. There we discover an important lesson in life, feeding our adversary creates the risks in all that we do.

There were other insights that did not appear so risky though educational. For example, one day my host took me to the Kennedy space station in Florida. This was a most amazing experience. Not only to see a spaceship prepared for a launch but also to be able to see inside some of the early space crafts and moon modules. I have never forgotten how small the cabins were and how close the astronauts had to be with each other. How important it must have been for the crew to get on well with each other. I was quite struck by that. It must have been something that they needed to work hard at as we can all have some annoying features about our selves. As Christians we also need to work hard at getting on well with each other. Jesus said "by this shall all men know that you are my disciples that you have love one for the other." What a challenge for us all, may we take up the challenge readily.

In Dallas came the opportunity to see the place where President Kennedy, or JFK as he was often called, was killed. John F. Kennedy was the 35th President of the United States of America, the youngest man elected to the office. On the 22nd November, 1963, when he was hardly past his first thousand days in office, JFK was assassinated in Dallas, Texas, becoming also the youngest President to die. Like many others of that period of time I will always remember where I was when JFK was killed. I had been to the cinema and returned home to hear the news from my dad. I could not believe it was true, at the same time I could not envisage there would be a time when I would stand on the very spot. Yet here I was. His Inaugural Address offered the memorable injunction: "Ask not what your country can do for you, ask what you can do for your country." I was reminded that Christians need to be addressing a similar challenge, "ask not what the church can do for you, ask what you can do for your church."

Conclusion

Thank you for following this journey of life with me. The late Cilla Black, or Priscilla White as she was initially known, once sang a song, "Life is full of surprises" and indeed it is. As you will have seen, the life of ministry does have its surprises as well and I have sought to reveal some of them. In ministry there is so much more that could be shared from the experiences of 41 years, but here are some for you to mull over at your leisure.

At this point as I come to a conclusion I would be amiss if I did not acknowledge my wife, Joan, and each of my children, Christianne, Suzanne, Philip, Elaine and Iain. They have been with me through so much and without their support the pages of this book would be very empty. Thank you for your support when it must have often been very difficult for you.

Thank you also to those who checked through certain parts of the book ensuring that sensitive details were not there. This is a vital part of the work of a book of this nature and I really appreciate the time that you gave.

Following on from that, thank you to Rev David Kinder for agreeing to write a foreword. I first met David when he was the Lead Chaplain of our local prison and he has some tremendous insights into the Prison Ministry. Thank you for all the time that you have put in. I wish you God's richest blessing in the midst of your retirement.

Finally, and not least, I must never forget to say thank you to my God who called me and equipped me despite my inadequacies. Nothing could be possible if it was not for the abilities God brings into the equation of life, and the promise of the Lord when he said He would never leave me nor forsake me, He will be with me till the end of the age.

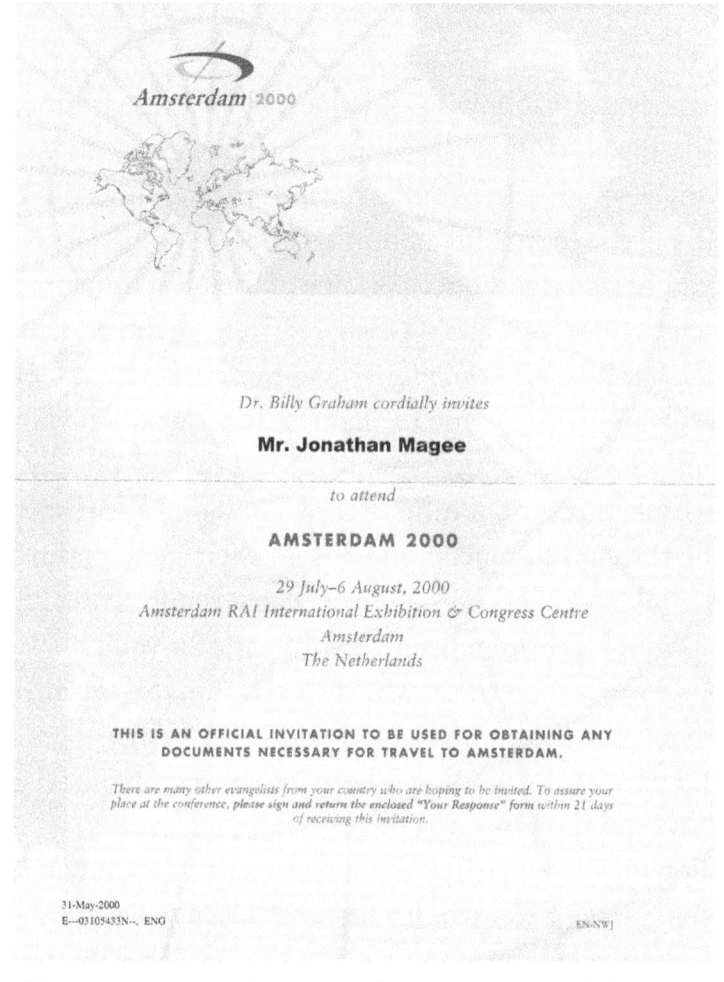

> Amsterdam 2000
>
> Dr. Billy Graham cordially invites
>
> **Mr. Jonathan Magee**
>
> to attend
>
> **AMSTERDAM 2000**
>
> 29 July–6 August, 2000
> Amsterdam RAI International Exhibition & Congress Centre
> Amsterdam
> The Netherlands
>
> THIS IS AN OFFICIAL INVITATION TO BE USED FOR OBTAINING ANY DOCUMENTS NECESSARY FOR TRAVEL TO AMSTERDAM.
>
> There are many other evangelists from your country who are hoping to be invited. To assure your place at the conference, please sign and return the enclosed "Your Response" form within 21 days of receiving this invitation.
>
> 31-May-2000
> E---03105433N--, ENG
> EN-NWJ

"Amsterdam2000, featured in the sequel following soon, More Confessions of a Baptist Minister"